# THE GREAT AGES OF WORLD ARCHITECTURE

BAROQUE AND ROCOCO   *Henry A. Millon*

CHINESE AND INDIAN   *Nelson I. Wu*

EARLY CHRISTIAN AND BYZANTINE   *William MacDonald*

GOTHIC   *Robert Branner*

GREEK   *Robert L. Scranton*

JAPANESE   *William Alex*

MEDIEVAL   *Howard Saalman*

MODERN   *Vincent Scully, Jr.*

PRE-COLUMBIAN   *Donald Robertson*

RENAISSANCE   *Bates Lowry*

ROMAN   *Frank E. Brown*

WESTERN ISLAMIC   *John D. Hoag*

# JAPANESE ARCHITECTURE

by William Alex

GEORGE BRAZILLER · NEW YORK · 1963

For Professor Jiro Murata

and

the wavers at the boat

# CONTENTS

# INTRODUCTION

Successive waves of culture that have washed across Japan from the mainland of Asia have strongly influenced but never significantly changed the basic Japanese racial character which seems to have crystallized some three thousand years ago. At that time, nature was the primary factor of existence for the Japanese and, in general, remained so until Japan was opened to the West about one hundred years ago. From the first coming of Buddhism in the sixth century A.D. until that time, the cultural evolvement of the Japanese had been a synthesis of their own ideals with the manifold cultural and religious forms of India, China, and Korea. It remains to be seen whether the Japanese can withstand or somehow divert the self-consuming materialism or the propensities for self-analysis characteristic of the "Westernization" process. The word "I" is a comparatively new one in Japan, still used with some discomfort.

The landscape of Japan harbors a concentration of nature at its most exotic: bubbling and steaming volcanic slopes, torrential streams and waterfalls, wild rock formations along the coasts, steep mountains inland, and great forests. During the past millennia Japan has had more than its share of earthquakes, typhoons, and tidal waves—again manifestations of nature whose effects were seemingly magnified because of the country's small size. Yet with a natural pleasure at the idea of being alive, a kind of gratitude tempered with elements of stoicism, the Japanese fitted themselves into the geologic faults—around the mountains and along the streams—considering themselves an intrinsic part of the total environment. It did not occur to them to do otherwise.

The early inhabitants assigned gods to all natural phenomena, life processes, and physical objects. The paramount deity was Amaterasu, the Sun Goddess, the source of life. She is worshiped at the Ise Inner Shrine, the holiest place in Japan. Second only to the Sun Goddess and worshiped a short distance away at an almost identical Outer Shrine, is Toyo-uke-bime, the Goddess of Food, for whom the early Japanese devised an offering, not of rich or elaborate gifts, but of what was really important: a sublimely nutritious diet consisting of four cups of water, sixteen saucers of rice, four saucers of salt, fish, fowl, fruits, sea-weed, and vegetables. Such was the quality of Shinto.

Buddhism was adopted in the eighth century as an official religion, accompanied by an unreserved acceptance of the culture attending it, a culture which involved the importation of new art forms, a complete system of religious and bureaucratic architecture, a new written language, even a means for salvation. Despite the power of Buddhism, the basic Japanese attitudes—a matter of the original intuitive emotionalism of Shinto—persisted, always expressed privately in the Japanese dwelling.

Japan is an amazing repository of Buddhism, having preserved major examples of Buddhist architecture of every historic period since its adoption. Great temple complexes were built after Chinese models with buildings symmetrically arranged on stone platforms, their columns painted vermillion, roof tiles brightly glazed—decisive architectural statements in disregard of nature, if not opposed to it. In time, this imported expression was considerably softened by the Japanese, whose own direct response to nature on the domestic level would consist of sliding open a series of room-height paper-covered partitions, for example, even in the dead of winter, to admire nature's landscape or its symbol, the garden, beside his house. Consisting of wood, thatch, rush, paper—a variety of vegetable products with mineral and ceramic accents—his house literally proclaimed nature; in addition, sliding interior partitions would have scenes or motifs from nature painted on them. The lack of physical warmth in winter is the necessarily passive quality, the stoic element, in so comprehensive a response to nature.

Originally from India, Zen Buddhism came to Japan in a later cultural wave, and brought doctrines close to those of Shinto. It denied a central motivating deity (Shinto also denied a single one by assignment of divinity to all things), maintained that the deepest truths of life were not susceptible to logic (in accord with unreflective, non-analytical qualities of Shinto beliefs), and instituted new mental disciplines toward everyday life, disdaining material desires (welcomed as providing clearly defined codes of personal behavior as well as condoning the use of simple natural materials rather than those hard to obtain). As the systematic in Zen reinforced the intuitive in Shinto, answering questions that Shinto, in a sense, had never really posed, imparting discipline and sophistication to the basic potential in nature's use, the domestic architecture of Japan came to yield an aesthetic return which continues to arouse world-wide admiration since its "discovery" in our time.

One component of the avid interest in Japanese forms may be a tacit sense of visual comfort. Japanese (and Asian) ways of seeing, or representing what one sees as a matter of how one feels about things, are very different from those of the West. The quality of depth in the East is perceived by concentric rather than linear means, by patterns, vistas, or groups of vistas, horizontally or vertically extended or behind each other, rather than by direct means of linear perspective. In paintings as well as in gardens, there is a sense of immediacy and enclosure rather than a falling away in depth via outgoing converging lines or planes. Infinity is not a focused collection of distant points but exists somewhere outside of a series of concentric spheres, varying in atmosphere and content, their boundaries never very well defined, their range to be taken in at one's own speed, according to one's own inclination. Reality is to be apprehended by a process which does not extend logic but which deepens emotion.

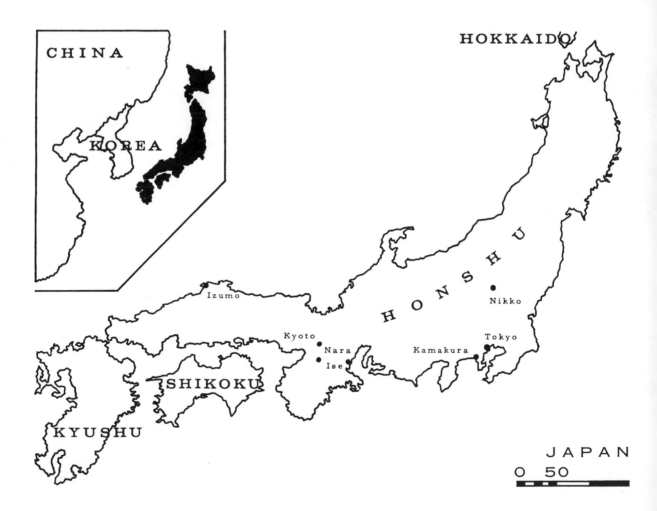

CHINA

KOREA

HOKKAIDO

HONSHU

Izumo

Nikko

Kyoto

Nara

Tokyo

Ise

Kamakura

SHIKOKU

KYUSHU

JAPAN

0  50

The first inhabitants of the Japanese Islands to whom an organized Stone Age culture may be ascribed were the Jomon people, who probably reached Japan from the north and central Asian mainland via Korea. Archaeological evidence shows that they used stone, bone, and shell implements in hunting, fishing, and "picking" edible wild grasses. They lived in rough huts constructed over shallow rectangular pits, excavated to a depth of about two to three feet (plate 1). Four posts or small trees set into holes near the inner edges of the pit supported lintel beams across them, and these in turn supported the roof structure (plate 2a). The general appearance was that of an elongated tent shape with a small ridged roof above it (plate 2b). The open ridge ends allowed smoke to escape. Lashed together and covered with bark and grass, the structure would seem able to withstand high winds and even earthquakes because of its altogether rational use of Stone Age materials. Sites in eastern and central Japan show variations in column arrangement and number, the enlargement of pit-dwellings by an outer range of postholes, and the use of drainage trenches at the perimeter. The conjectured reconstruction shown is typical of *tateana* dwellings, as these pit-houses are called, of some three thousand years ago. These dwellings were arranged in large groups, probably for protection, indicating the existence of fairly stable communities. Apart from their dwellings, the Jomon achieved one of the highest artistic levels of any neolithic culture. The word Jomon itself means "rope-pattern," a name derived from the characteristic rope coils and patterns with which their earthenware was decorated.

A second immigration or invasion (also by way of Korea) brought the Yayoi people, named after the location in Tokyo where their first archaeological remains were found. Southeast Asian or Oceanic derivation seems indicated by their architectural preference for high-floor or pile-supported dwellings. In addition to the artistic excellence in the design and decoration of their artifacts, the Yayoi had special stone-working techniques, an organized architectural system, and probably the use of bronze. These give evidence of a culture superior to that of the Jomon whom they dominated and absorbed. With the advent of the Yayoi, the landscape began to take on a more civilized character. Whereas Jomon groups of pit-houses were often located on hillside ridges and other sites appropriate for defense, Yayoi settlements occurred in the lower midlands, which were more suitable for crop irrigation, especially for the cultivation of rice.

Incised designs on bronze objects and earthenware from about the second to the fifth century A.D., as well as clay house-miniatures, provide the earliest architectural representations. An earthenware specimen excavated from a site near Nara shows a high-floor house with steps or a ladder leading up to it, the roof apparently a simple gable form with a pronounced outward inclination at both ends (plate 3a). The same type of house picture, incised on a contemporary bronze object, shows a platform below the roof and the rafters exposed in an "exploded" graphic representation. Noteworthy is the extension of the rafters above and beyond the horizontal ridge beam which itself extends beyond the building proper, on the short sides where it is supported by posts (plate 3b). Evidence in greater detail is shown on the back of a bronze mirror of the fifth century[1] found at Sumida, near Nara (plate 4), which is decorated with four structures, two of them variations of high-floor dwellings, one possibly a "ground-level" house, the last a pit-dwelling. The most elaborate design, which seems to have a balcony around it, has broad wood-plank walls set between posts in the upper story and smaller planks of bound rushes or wood "woven" into a chevron pattern in the story below. The second presumed dwelling is a smaller, simpler version of the first; the others may be a granary and a peasant's field house. The discovery of numbers of clay *haniwa* house models in contemporary tombs may indicate that wealth in the form of stored grain and goods was thereby symbolized (only a rich and noble chieftain would have a tomb), and the bronze mirror may have represented an architectural estate. Thus, a *haniwa* house with four small pavilions attached (plate 5a) may signify a dwelling with its storehouses. It is fairly certain that *haniwa* houses with *katsuogi*, the ridge-crossing cylinders (plate 5b), represented noble dwellings, the others probably their accompanying store- or treasure-houses. The original function of these crosspieces cannot be assigned, for although they may have been used in securing rafter ends or roofing thatch to the ridge beams, they were actually quite unnecessary for this. In any case, they later became a mark of Imperial status reserved for Imperial architecture or Shinto shrines, both of which shared an identity that was symbolic as well as physical in that the Emperor was custodian of certain precious objects symbolizing the presence of Shinto gods.[2]

Surprisingly inconsistent with the modest shrinelike dwellings of the Emperors (the word palace seems inappropriate) were the

16

Imperial tombs. The largest, that of Emperor Nintoku who reigned at the beginning of the fifth century, is some 1600 feet long (plate 6). Surrounded by three separate moats, its central tumulus, which is over 100 feet high, is said to shelter the main vault. In the latter part of the eighteenth century a portion of the square front caved in, disclosing a stone chamber in which were seen a sarcophagus, iron armor, and glass vessels.[3] Now covered with trees, the tomb was originally partially paved with masonry blocks; the mound and moats were ringed with rows of *haniwa* sculptures, simple but remarkably expressive clay figurines and animals set into the earth to prevent erosion of the tomb. Twelve smaller Imperial tombs in the vicinity of Nintoku's, varying somewhat in size and shape, demonstrate considerable material and human resources expended in devotion to the Emperors or at least under their command. Large-scale Imperial mound burial ended under the influence of Buddhism in the seventh century.

By the fourth century the central authority of the Imperial clan was clearly established in Japan. An active relationship with the continent through Korea, although primarily political and military, brought a cultural stimulus which increased with the passage of time and was marked in the fifth century by the importation and acceptance of Chinese as the official language.

An air view of pre-Buddhist Japan, say from the third to the fifth century, would show (in addition to Imperial burial mounds) pastoral scenes of highly organized agricultural communities, coastal fishing villages, district centers with clan headquarters elaborated for defense and prestige, as well as occasional shrine complexes near unusual "concentrations" of nature such as waterfalls, caves, rock formations, mountain tops, or forest glens. A vague mythology mixing with an inchoate pantheism had gradually become organized into Shinto—"the way of the gods"—and natural sites with an air of grandeur or mystery about them, obviously where the gods would be, became places of early Shinto worship. These were places of adoration and identification, not of fear, for in Shinto the universe and all existence, including man, were related and therefore partook of divinity. Unconcerned with conjectural or analytical religious philosophies, it was a dynamic religion, dominating and unifying the national subconscious and concerned directly with nature as divinity manifest everywhere—in trees, organic life, the earth, and in the natural phenomena of birth, growth, and decay. Within this framework were founded the attitudes toward the architectural use of natural materials, attitudes which have persisted to the present day.

The Ise Shrines, the holiest in Japan, have been generally preserved as they were when originally built in the third and fourth centuries. Using natural growing things symbolic of Shinto, the craftsmen of that time created a pure architecture in expression of their spiritual ideal. Their materials and structure are similar to those of the high-floor dwellings previously discussed; the Ise sanctuaries are dwellings of the most refined sort, for the most important Shinto divinities. They are not a vast and permanent monument but a living part of their environment. The buildings are torn down every twenty years and new ones are built on an immediately adjacent site. The new Shrines, although identical with the old ones, are not considered a *replica* of Ise, but are Ise *re-created*, in a process revealing Shinto's understanding of nature which does not make monuments but lives and dies, always renewed and reborn.

The buildings of Ise are set in the midst of a forest of ancient and lofty Cryptomeria trees; the Shrines consist of two similar complexes about four miles apart. The first, called the Naiku, or Inner Shrine, is dedicated to the Sun Goddess Amaterasu-o-mi-kami; and the second, called Geku, or Outer Shrine, was built in the fourth century for Toyo-uke-bime-no-kami, the Goddess of Food. The Naiku complex (plates 7–15) is enclosed by an outer fence measuring about 370 feet on the sides and 200 feet at the ends. Inner fences are arranged so as to give an increasing sense of enclosure up to the Shoden, the main sanctuary (plates 10, 11), which contains the Sacred Mirror. A late nineteenth-century drawing shows the Shoden at the rear of the enclosure with the Honden, or treasure houses, immediately adjacent on either side (plate 9). These were moved to the rear in a subsequent rebuilding.

18

The building material of Ise is the *hinoki* tree, a species of Japanese white cypress, used throughout for posts, beams, framing, and boards. It is planed smooth and then left in its natural state. The roofs, which shed Japan's heavy rainfall, are built up in a delicate curve from strips of *hinoki* bark and then trimmed. A conventionalization of the fundamental upright —the tree—is seen in the round supporting posts which are set directly into the ground, while beams, as more obviously man-made additions, are squared—both in complete structural and visual accord. Structure is visible everywhere and no surfaces are painted. The inseparability of a decorative effect from its functional origin is seen in the gold caps of the *katsuogi*, which protect their weather-vulnerable ends. Although slight modifications occurred under Buddhist influence during the Nara Period (645–793), as seen in the decorative brass ornaments of the Shoden's balustrade and steps (plate 10), the Shrines and their accompanying buildings, varying in size but sharing the same architectural expression, are pure Shinto. A completely unselfconscious masterpiece in wood and thatch, Ise is truly unique among the world's buildings for the spiritually architectonic quality it achieves.

The shrine building style of Ise, called Shimmei, is followed by many lesser shrines throughout Japan. Typical among them is the Shimmeigu Shrine (plate 16) located in Nagano Prefecture in west central Honshu. The buildings closely resemble those of Ise but, nestling in a quiet forest grove, have a relaxed provincial air about them, as is generally the case at small shrines where worship—except for special days and festivals—is a casual, individual affair. On the western coast of the same province is the oldest and second most important shrine in Japan, Izumo (plate 17).

Believed to date from as far back as the first century, Izumo Shrine "was built in the same shape as the Emperor's palace," according to ancient records, and does relate directly in its architectural style to high-floor dwellings of the archaic period. The sanctuary, thought to have been originally much higher and larger than its present size of some thirty feet square (exclusive of its high surrounding balcony), shows in plan (plate 19) a central post reminiscent of the cosmologically significant central pillar found in the primitive architecture of Oceania.[4] Its walls are broad wood planks set between posts. Under Buddhist influence during various rebuildings, the roof was made curved and the *chigi*, or crossing gable-end boards forming a V shape, became merely vestigial elements set on the ridge behind the decorative ridge-end ornament. The entrance is set off to one side as would be the case in an archaic dwelling with a central, gable-end post (plate 18). The Izumo and Ise shrine styles served as the basis for two later shrine-style variations which were characterized by curved and flowing roofs. The Kasuga style (plate 20), stemming from Izumo, and the widespread Nagare style (plate 21), based on the Ise type, both appeared during the Nara Period at the height of the first peak of Chinese Buddhist temple building. From about 3,000 shrines recorded at that time the

*19*

number has grown enormously. Some are very small with just one shrine building and its *torii*,[5] but others are great complexes dedicated to several Shinto deities and containing many subsidiary buildings in their precincts (plate 22).

According to the *Nihongi*, an official early-eighth-century chronicle, an embassy from the King of Paikche (in Korea) brought in the year 552 a statue of Buddha, sutra scrolls, and other Buddhist paraphernalia as gifts to the Japanese Emperor together with a message commending the new religion. At first, the adoption of the new belief was a tentative process, becoming a matter of court and clan rivalries, causing a civil war in 587, but gradually winning favor as the nobility found it a welcome intellectual and emotional stimulus. Later embassies from Korea, usually appeals for military assistance, also brought Buddhist monks in increasing numbers together with relics, books, and art, as well as artisans of all sorts—temple carpenters, sculptors, scribes, and other purveyors of the continental culture. Buddhism found its champion in the energetic Prince Shotoku Taishi (572–621), who may be called its true founder in Japan. Its appeal to him was philosophical; he saw in its doctrines the benefits of highly organized moral, religious, and social codes. He promulgated the new faith with an impressive panoply of ritual, iconography, and architecture. By the time of his death, there existed in Japan 48 Buddhist temples attended by 820 priests. He laid the groundwork so well that by the end of that century there were over 550 temples.

The first Japanese examples closely followed the current mainland models of Korean and Chinese Buddhist temple compounds. In line on the major south-to-north axis were the outer south gate, then the inner gate marking the southern end of the rectangular enclosure, next the pagoda seen first in the courtyard with the "Buddha" hall directly behind it, finally the lecture hall centered at the north end of the compound. Additional buildings were placed on axis north of the enclosure.

The Horyuji Temple near Nara, originally founded by Prince Shotoku in 607, was completely destroyed by fire and rebuilt toward the end of the seventh century. From this rebuilding it still retains the Middle Gate (Chumon) of the enclosing rectangular corridor, the five-tiered Pagoda (Gojunoto) and the Main Hall (Kondo), the oldest known wooden buildings in the world (plates 23–27). Their arrangement departs from the continental rule of axial balance which had previously been followed, thus providing early evidence of a change in religious preference and, possibly, of the Japanese taste for asymmetry.

Placed on either side of the main axis, both the Kondo and Pagoda are immediately visible to one entering the courtyard and are expressed as individual buildings rather than as elements in an architectural hierarchy directly reflecting a religious one. The pagoda,[6] in spite of its important function of housing Buddha relics, was shifted about in later temple plans because of the difficulty in relating its form to the other buildings within the compound. Later, pairs of pagodas were built within the enclosure as well as outside of it. On the other hand the Kondo, housing holy images of Buddha, came to occupy the place of prominence at the center of the enclosure.

Temples at this time were built as monastic colleges more intent on teaching the faith than in disseminating it to a gathered assemblage. But as general interest in their activities grew, they were required to expand and adapt. Strict adherence to continental architectural ideals became impossible, had this been desirable, and so-called "pure" buildings are rare. If adaptation did not take place in construction, it occurred later for various reasons: transfer of temples from one site to another, rebuilding after destruction (whether by fire or other causes—political in turbulent later centuries), often to accommodate changing ritual and the achievement of newly desired religious effects—not to speak of structural innovations for purely visual reasons. Both Kondo and Pagoda at Horyuji (plates 24–26) have had their lower stories enlarged by the addition of roofed porches masking the lower walls and their supporting columns, softening considerably the original structural vigor of the buildings and yet supplanting this with an agreeable feeling of repose. Graceful proportions impart a monumentality much beyond the comparatively modest scale of the buildings. Typical columns can be seen in the Chumon (plate 27), their entasis a possible result of Greek influence traveling across Asia.[7]

Contemporary Chinese T'ang Dynasty influence is preserved in the Hokkedo, another of the rare relics of the early Nara Period located at Todaiji Temple (plate 28). The Hokkedo is a simple chapel which has remained largely intact except for a later addition at one end, It shows a low roof slope and general proportions consistents with Chinese prototypes—a straightforward use of the structural system of columns, lintel beams, and corbelled-out multiple brackets. In the Hokkedo, the bracketing system is employed clearly, extending laterally in the wall plane to support horizontal beams, projecting perpendicularly from the building to support the rafters (plate 30), and, on the interior, giving substantial support to the coved ceiling (plate 29).

The Kondo of Toshodaiji Temple was built for an illustrious Chinese Buddhist monk named Ganjin, who was brought to Japan after great difficulty and given sole powers of priestly ordination by the Emperor. Although subsequent rebuildings seem to have raised the roof and given it a steeper slope, the Kondo is an excellent example of fully developed Nara Period architecture (plate 31). Its plaster wall panels are screens set between columns, giving the same façade appearance inside and out. Windows are vertical wood lattice bars. Generously dimensioned and showing much greater refinement than the Hokkedo, the structure is seven bays wide and four deep, of which the first bay is a colonnade (plates 32, 33). Column entasis is much less marked than in the early Nara period. The colonnade tie beams are carved so as to make them seem to swell upward into arch forms, a dynamic quality shared by the interior spanning members or "rainbow" beams as they are called. The coffered polychromed ceiling forms a canopy for a sixteen-foot-high Vairocana Buddha with his attendants (plate 34).

The Golden Age of Buddhism reached its climax, however, some years before the building of Toshodaiji, with the Todaiji Monastery, which was founded in 745, marking the complete adoption of Buddhism as a state religion by the Imperial House. Todaiji was the largest, most powerful monastery in Japan, larger in fact than anything the Chinese had. Building the Hall of the Great Buddha in the center of a two-square-mile enclosure, with gates, pagodas, subsidiary buildings, and colonnades, as well as casting the great bronze Buddha itself, was a monumental event of great national importance and expense.[8] Presently two thirds its original size, but nevertheless the largest wooden building in the world under one roof, the Daibutsuden, Hall of the Great Buddha, measures 188 feet along the front, 166 feet on the sides and 157 feet in height (plates 35–41). It contains the largest bronze statue in the world, a $53\frac{1}{2}$-foot-high seated figure of the Vairocana Buddha (plate 41), to whom the building was dedicated by the Emperor Shomu in 752. The Daibutsuden's present architectural style, adopted during the rebuilding of

1180, is called Tenjikuyo, based on the Sung Chinese construction methods used by the priest Chogen, in charge of its reconstruction. Its outstanding quality is the bracketing system which extends up and outward in one plane (plate 37)—in the case of the lower eave about 30 feet from the building. Now missing four of its original front bays, thus shorter by some 100 feet but almost the same height, the Daibutsuden seems strangely proportioned, its Buddha somewhat cramped. An entrance detail reproduced from a twelfth-century Japanese scroll painting (plate 39) recalls a more generous monumentality, closer to the forceful religious feeling it must have evoked when it was the central fact of Buddhism in Japan.

Standing behind the Daibutsuden to the northwest is the Imperial Repository, or Shosoin, established in 745 (plates 42, 43). It accommodates the royal collection of artistic and ceremonial objects with their related documents, as well as many personal belongings of Emperor Shomu. (A comparable heritage for the Western world would be the treasures of Charlemagne preserved intact and fully catalogued.) Through twelve centuries of often tumultuous Japanese history, the building has remained inviolate, its three openings sealed with slips of paper on which each succeeding Emperor simply writes his name. Except for its tile roof, the Shosoin is built completely of wood, its form undoubtedly derived from the earlier wood-plank, high-floor granaries. It is not known whether the building was put up as a single unit or was originally two separate storehouses connected by a later addition between them. Similar and approximately contemporary treasure houses standing side by side at Toshodaiji Temple (plate 44) lead to the latter supposition. In the Shosoin, however, there are three separate sections each with its own set of doors. Forty massive *hinoki* logs in ten rows support the 108-foot-long windowless building, its end sections built up of triangular hewn timbers laid lengthwise and crossed at the corners, with no caulking between. The excellent preservation of the treasures seems due to the walls, expanding and closing during wet weather, thus keeping moisture out, and contracting during dry weather, so that fresh air may circulate within—a uniquely organic time capsule. The treasures are taken out anyway for a ceremonial airing once a year.[9]

Following the broad "scholastic" Buddhism of the Nara Period came the importation of newer, more intricate forms of Buddhism: the "esoteric" Tendai and Shingon cults of the Heian

23

Period (794–1185). Imperial support was granted these sects at about the same time that the capital was moved from Nara to Heian-kyo, now Kyoto, partly to obviate the growing political power of the Nara monasteries, especially Todaiji. Initially both new sects required isolated mountain sites where small, informally arranged halls were scaled down to the performance of disciplined rites in a spirit of religious reform contrasting with Nara's current laxity. As the Buddhist pantheon grew complex, expanding to become identified occasionally with Shinto divinities, there began a kind of nationalization process architecturally descriptive of a more "native" Buddhism. This process of amalgamation was the reverse of that seen earlier with the use of curved roof shapes, brass ornamentation, and other Buddhist architectural characteristics in Shinto shrines.

An example of the new tendency is preserved in the Muroji Temple (plates 45–47) of the early Heian Period, located in Nara Prefecture. Beside their other qualities as Shingon buildings, both Kondo and Pagoda, in an informal wooded setting, are roofed with *hinoki* bark shingles. The Pagoda, otherwise conventional in structure, is quite small, perhaps as an early example of Shingon modesty, only 53 feet high. The Sambutsuji Temple (plate 48), possibly at the outside architectural range of esoteric Buddhist temple building, is remarkable for its mountain-side site (suggestive of Shinto). Located in Tottori Prefecture, its precise date is uncertain but aspects of its elegant architectural detailing place it in the Heian Period. Examples like these are not to suggest that formal temple arrangements based on the original T'ang Chinese style were abandoned. They continued to be built by the Imperial House and the wealthy aristocracy, often as conspicuously elaborate expressions of faith, on appropriate level sites in urban or near-urban areas. Esoteric cult temples were also built in more usual locations as Tendai and Shingon Buddhism grew in popularity and power. Both sects also made extensive use of a pagoda which was closer in architectural form to the classic *stupa* of Indian derivation (*Cf.* note 6). Serving as physical demonstrations of Buddhist cosmological doctrines, and also as reliquaries, Tahoto pagodas adapted both Indian and Chinese forms, resulting in a Japanese version with rectangular lower stories and partially visible dome vestiges of plaster, all covered over with a sloping square roof. Although no Heian examples exist, the Pagoda at Kongosanmaiin Temple (plate 49), built during the Kamakura Period (1186–1335), illustrates this Japanese form.

24

Jodo, a third important Buddhist sect which arose during Heian times, was one of the simplest, centering around belief in the powers of Amida Buddha, who would take all to paradise—this faith to be expressed, according to the most accommodating interpretation, by repetition of the *nembutsu*, a three-word formula (*Namu Amida Butsu*) in homage to Amida. Worship in the hall containing his image consisted in part of continuous recitation of the formula while walking around the statue, which was located in the central bay. The late Heian Period Shiramizu Amidado typifies the simplest kind of Jodo hall in straightforward native taste, as it were (plates 50–52), while at the other extreme (the appeal of Jodo was all-inclusive) the Byodoin Hoodo (plates 53–56) transforms the Amida Hall into a luxuriant scene commensurate, by way of its opulent brilliance, with the promised paradise itself. First a villa, later made into a temple by the Fujiwara clan members who by that time governed Japan in the Emperor's name, the Hoodo was the gilded, mother-of-pearl background for ceremonies richly evocative of paradise. The easy recitation of the *nembutsu* was indeed a far cry, especially in such surroundings, from the disciplined metaphysical search for the path of true Buddhist enlightenment. Fronting on a lotus lake, the Hoodo's wood exterior is painted vermilion; its form relates to the Shinden style of dwelling to be discussed later.

During the Kamakura Period the three main styles of Buddhist temple building were: Tenjikuyo, the style used in reconstructing (during Kamakura times) the Todaiji Daibutsuden, previously shown, as well as in other buildings identified with the priest Chogen; Wayo, the continuation of Heian esoteric cult Buddhist styles; and the new Karayo, the architecture which was carefully imported by Zen Buddhism and which originally followed Sung Dynasty Chinese forms of strict symmetry, again on a central axis. In time the two latter styles merged to form a basis for all later temple building. The complex developments within each style are too numerous to mention here although, generally, much Japanese structural ingenuity was expended in combining separate lay assembly halls and sanctuaries into one building. During this process, while ceiling heights were kept the same, the roof was almost invariably raised and frequently covered with thatch or cypress bark shingles. The intermediate roof framework used additional cantilever eave supports, which tended to remove structural justification for the bracketing, which in turn moved toward a less functional, more decorative use. A dramatic example of the preoccupation with roofs is shown in the Zen Buddhist Engakuji Shariden, or Reliquary Hall, which has in place of its low, tile predecessor, a very fine, high, soberly decorative roof of thatch (plates 57–59).

Until the beginning of the eighth century the death of the Emperor was cause for vacating his residence (in effect the capital); the succeeding Emperor thereupon had a new dwelling built on an auspicious site where, with some inconvenience, the entire court and bureaucracy were required to move their residences or rebuild them. On the accession of Emperor Gemmei in 708 Nara was chosen (and remained) capital for a 75-year period which included seven consecutive reigns. In spite of its limited duration as capital, Nara was a symbol of political maturity, a permanent center of administration, as well as the religious and cultural nucleus of Japan, until compelling reasons forced a move to the site of Kyoto in 793.[10] The new capital, Heian-kyo (Capital of Peace and Tranquility), like Nara before it, was laid out according to the plan of Ch'ang-an, the renowned capital of T'ang China.

Heian-kyo, now called Kyoto, then measured three and one half miles from north to south and three miles from east to west, its main and lesser streets crisscrossing to form a gridiron pattern (plate 63). The administrative bureaus, ceremonial halls, and Imperial Palace were situated within a large enclosure on the axial center, dominating the entire city from the north (plate 61). Around and below the official compound were temple and shrine precincts, aristocratic estates with their mansions enclosed behind high walls, and the houses of the ordinary inhabitants. It is estimated that at the end of the eighth century there were one hundred thousand houses and one half million people. Most of the buildings in the original administrative enclosure, which measured about one mile long by three quarters of a mile wide, were magnificently decorated—their red pillars set in white plaster and their roofs covered with blue glazed tiles, patterned after Chinese forms. Apart from the state and administrative halls, the palace complex covered approximately one twenty-fifth of the enclosure (plate 60). Its plan follows Chinese models but its architecture, providing a properly restrained background for the aesthetically inclined court of Heian times, was essentially Japanese. The present buildings are a reconstruction made in 1854. The most important of these are the Shishinden, or Front Hall of Audience, and the Seiryoden, the apartments of the Emperor.

Bound to the strict symmetry of Chinese prototypes, the Shishinden is directly on axis with the central gate. The rectangular court before it is completely enclosed by arcades which extend from the gate around to its sides (plate 62). This captive space, given direction by a floor of raked sand, brings the eye to the superb elevation of the Shishinden (plate 65). Its *moya*, or main room, which originally served as an audience hall, is now the place of enthronement of the Emperors of Japan. It is approached from the front through two verandas; the inner one, typical of the interior with its satin-smooth floors of *hinoki* and plaster upper walls, is marked off by rows of round columns (plate 66). The throne dais is in the center of the *moya*. Between the columns of the outer row hang vertical *shitomido*, or paper-covered wooden lattices, later adopted for the exterior walls of Shinden mansions. Swung up into a horizontal position, they open the entire building; closed, they become the interior façade. A less definite degree of separation is attained with use of *sudare*, thin, roll-up bamboo shades, suspended just outside the *shitomido* and also between the columns of the inner row. The structure is everywhere clearly evident; the dressed beams of the interior are exposed right up to the ridge.

Directly northwest of the Shishinden and connected to it by a short open corridor is the Seiryoden, or Serene and Cool Hall, originally designed and used as the Emperor's dwelling, but later converted to ceremonial purposes. (Plate 67 shows the *shitomido* lowered in the left façade.) Similar to the Shishinden in construction, it also has double front verandas but differs in proportion and plan, having several small apartments and receiving rooms, the largest of which is the Emperor's living room. The special mats for sitting, used for the Emperor's formal dinner, are located so as to afford a view of the court (plate 69). To the left of these mats is the Sekkaidan, a plaster rectangle polished with beeswax which, during inclement weather, was spread with earth for the Emperor to stand on as required in performance of certain Shinto rituals (plate 70). Sunk into the plaster is a circular hearth covered with a convex copper disc. A twelfth-century scroll painting shows a scene before the Seiryoden, the inner *sudare* lowered, due to the Emperor's illness, while courtiers leaning against veranda posts receive a report from an Imperial

27

messenger seated on the ground. The Sekkaidan is behind the *sudare* on the left (plate 68).

The walls of the corridors which bound the raked sand courts are made of white plaster sections built up on bamboo lath between squared wooden framing members. Dark squares within each bay are sliding wooden screens which protect paper-covered inner screens directly behind them (plate 72). The architectonic discipline of this court must have been an admirable foil for the colorful costumes of participants in the archery contests, musical performances, and ceremonials that took place within it.

The Shishinden, together with its forecourt, presented the classical, reserved appearance befitting an Imperial palace, albeit on a small scale. The buildings behind it, however, tended to break down into a characteristic informality of plan (in contrast to strict Chinese ideals which required symmetrically united fronts against evil forces from any direction). In detail and materials, from the raised wood floor to the *hinoki* bark roof shingles, the palace was indigenously Japanese.

The Shinden style of dwelling developed in Heian times when the court nobility, given rectangular plots of land around and below the Imperial enclosure (size according to rank), based the construction of their houses on the same Chinese ancestry as the Imperial Palace and, like the Palace, demonstrated an initial symmetry of left to right but not of front to rear. The mansion-estate centered about the chief dwelling, or Shinden, which faced south to an open court (plate 73). Attached by two sets of covered wide corridors, *watadono*, were the east and west *tainoya*, or subsidiary living quarters. From these, narrow corridors extending to the south ended in small pavilions, *tsuridono*, which completed the U-shape arrangement around the court. Wealthier nobles built additional buildings behind the front rank of Shinden and *tainoya*, while lesser nobles might not have even the basic complement of buildings. The main, clear-span room of the Shinden, called *moya* (plate 74), was surrounded by a secondary roofed space called *hisashi*. The narrow outermost veranda was permitted a railing if the owner had sufficient rank. The *moya* was not partitioned but usually contained a small enclosed bedchamber of sturdy clay-wall or wood-plank construction. Visual privacy was otherwise secured by use of low portable screens. Thick rectangular *tatami*-type mats were placed on the wooden floor for permanent seating, while conveniently portable round mats were used casually throughout.

Across the court from the *moya* one could see the pond garden (forming the southern limit of the walled enclosure) with its islands linked by miniature bridges. Mountain shapes, trees, rocks, and lanterns combined into a landscaped representation of the Amida Buddha's paradise of the West (to which one was transported in the Amida's boat). To supply the pond, a small stream was led through the grounds from the north under the right-side *watadono*, which was appropriately arched. Standing over the pond at the southern terminal of the corridors, *tsuridono*, really tastefully refined bowers, served as landing stages for boating parties, pavilions from which to watch the moon or snow landscape, or simply as cool places to compose poems. The more businesslike part of the Shinden centered around the east gate—the formal entrance—where officers and guards were quartered.

Reconstruction from old records and scroll paintings of the Fujiwara clan Shinden, Tosanjoden, shows a departure from the usual plan: there is no *tainoya* on the west. The large eastern one is directly connected to an extensive reception complex of guards' quarters, waiting rooms for retainers of noble visitors, stables, etc. (plate 75). The plan is of significant interest for the future of "domestic" architecture in its tendency toward a compact, echelon type of building arrangement. This was emphasized in smaller Shindens where, as time progressed, corridors were gradually shortened until they disappeared, and the outbuildings came to be attached to the chief dwelling. During the progress of the Heian into the Kamakura Period, there was an increasing use of sliding partitions, rather than physical distance, to differentiate living areas. As the multiple functions of dwellings were concentrated in adjacent buildings, the central round columns of the *moya* became square to accord visually with the other interior columns designed to receive sliding wood partition-doors or the lighter *fusuma* panels, made of paper-covered wood framework. The interior of a developed (and rather noble) Shinden is shown in an early fourteenth-century scroll as having floors completely covered with *tatami* and making extensive use of decorated sliding partitions. Elements of the original central Shinden can be seen: the narrow wooden veranda, lowered *sudare* and *shitomido* (now in two sections, the lower removable, the upper hinged) of the first plane of closure; the *hisashi* area ending in a row of columns resting on a floor plate which separates the rows of *tatami*, rolled-up *sudare* at this plane providing the second degree of closure; and the *moya* itself where two noblemen are conversing (plate 76). The modular unit of plan for purposes of column spacing was the *tatami*, somewhat larger at first than its now generally stable dimensions of six by three feet. A view of the Shinden dwelling of a lower-ranking nobleman has much more of a domestic quality about it, showing mats only partially covering the floor, the interior a bit crowded with people and furniture, and indications that the stable, although perhaps not under the same roof, was extremely close by (plate 77). A warrior's house on the southern island of Kyushu, during the later Kamakura era, shows a simplified "Shinden" with just a narrow wooden veranda separating the pavilion interior from a small court: the place in the *moya* reserved for more auspicious occasions designated by an inner row of *tatami* (plate 78). An archer's tower over the wood-plank stockade gate points up the military character of the times.

When Japan entered a period of military feudalism the Fujiwara clan, which had ruled through cleverness, wealth, and intermarriage with the Imperial house, was replaced by the powerful Tiara family. The Tiara were soon vanquished by the Minamoto clan, which instituted the Shogunate system of regency, leaving the Emperor at Kyoto (now become the ceremonial capital of Japan) while real power—based on the wealth of vast feudal estates which supported formidable armies—emanated from the ruling capital at Kamakura, three hundred miles away. However, the dwelling styles during this time were based on the Kyoto Shinden, modified as necessary for the nobility or the warrior class. The disciplined military of Kamakura found certain aspects of one Buddhist cult directly consonant with their own doctrines. This was Zen Buddhism, which in time penetrated every aspect of Japanese life but had the immediate effect of setting forth clear lessons of social behavior, not only with regard to personal military loyalty, but in the art of daily life.

Some of the formative elements of Japanese domestic architecture, which was stabilized at about the end of the fifteenth century, made their appearance during the Kamakura Period. Among the most important of these, deriving from Zen Buddhist chapel-dwellings, were the *tokonoma* and *shoin*. The *tokonoma* developed from the private altar in a priest's house where a low, narrow wood table with an incense burner, votive candles, and flower vessels was placed before a Buddhist scroll painting hung on the wall. Later a built-in alcove was devoted to this arrangement. Still later it was used for the display of paintings and art objects. The *shoin* was a windowed desk alcove for study built out onto the wood veranda of a priestly dwelling (plate 86). Also a Zen Buddhist element, it found its way into the mainstream of secular architecture like a status symbol, lending a scholarly air to what became the main guest room. A third element was the previous freestanding "book case" for scrolls and other objects which became *tana*, built-in wall storage shelves, some open, others covered with sliding doors. The Shoin style of domestic architecture was the name given to the combined use of these elements in the characteristic central room of the Japanese house.[11] Frequently the importance of this room was emphasized by raising part of its floor one step above the main floor; this platform was called *jodan*, the room then called *odanoma*.

The gradual development of this architectural style occurred during the Muromachi Period (1336–1573), when Kyoto once again became the real capital of Japan under the Ashikaga Shoguns. Aside from considerable political unrest, this regency was marked by two outstanding characteristics: a general artistic resurgence nurtured by the zealous aestheticism of the various Shoguns (reminiscent of Heian times), and their strong support of the Zen priesthood because the latter gave much needed advice in all matters from the tea ceremony to civil administration. Two important examples of Ashikaga architectural taste are found in Kyoto. The first, Shogun Yoshimitsu's retirement temple-villa, the Kinkaku (plate 79), was built at the end of the fourteenth century and recently was rebuilt after being burned. Placed at the edge of a pleasant lake in whose reflection its delicate ambiance is gently diffused, the Kinkaku was perfectly suited to the aesthetic pursuits of Yoshimitsu who could retire for meditation, when he wished, to the Zen chapel which formed its upper story. Its reflective qualities were particularly enhanced by the gold leaf which covered parts of the interior and exterior.

Of the large Shoin mansion called Higashiyamaden, built by the later Shogun Yoshimasa in the fifteenth century, two buildings remain: the Ginkaku, or "Silver Pavilion" (plate 80), intended to be a counterpart to the Kinkaku but never covered with silver foil, and the Togudo (plates 82–85), one part of which is a Buddhist chapel and the other, the oldest existing example of Shoin architecture, in the form of a small tea-ceremony room.

31

The Togudo has both *shoin* and *tana* (plate 83) in its four-and-one-half-mat tea room but lacks a *tokonoma*, its use possibly precluded at this early age by an adjunct function in the chapel part of the building. Given Yoshimasa's impetus, Teaism, long known in Japan as a "practice" or ritual, became a cult as well as a genuine instrument of culture. Its effect on architecture, especially the Shoin style, will be seen later.

What Westerners call the Japanese house is the Shoin style of dwelling. By the sixteenth century, its conventional use of structure, materials, and room arrangement in plan (or more properly speaking, the principles of plan) was generally typical of the most extensive palace as well as of the smallest tea house; the same use persists today. The strata of people in Japan occupying the middle class around the year 1600—court scholars, minor nobility, samurai chieftains, and priests— lived in houses, with appropriate modifications, like the Kojoin Kyakuden, specifically a priest's guest house, at the Onjoji Temple (plates 87–93).[12]

It is made of wood, Japan's chief building material since the beginning of its architectural history. In plan, the Kyakuden recalls the oblong Shinden-style *moya*; the roofed porch extending from one corner is a vestige of the Shinden corridor system. Structurally a tightly joined skeleton frame of post-and-beam construction, the Kyakuden is raised about two feet above the ground, with each of its floor posts resting on a small foundation stone. This prevents moisture from rotting the column bases, a functional necessity in a land of heavy rainfall; and during Japan's frequent earthquakes the system enables the structure to bounce, as a chair would, whereas a building with columns set into the ground could be twisted and broken. The method of column spacing accords with the modular system determined by the number of *tatami* desired in a room and allows a versatile use of interior space as well as a free choice of exterior openings. This is in contrast to the fixed spaces of solid wall construction. Artistry in roof design combines with the requirements of building orientation, producing an eave system which allows winter sun to penetrate the interior while excluding the hot rays of summer sun as well as oblique rainfall. The Kyakuden's roof of *hinoki* bark strips is the Irimoya type of hipped roof with gable ends, gracefully intersected by the small gable roof of the porch whose eave line swells up to form a Chinese style (*kara-hafu*) gable above the entrance (plate 90). The veranda circling the building is accessible through sliding exterior screens, *shoji*, made of thin wood lath covered on the outside with a tough translucent paper. In summer these are often removed, completely opening the house to the outside, a desirable arrangement in Japan because of the extreme humidity, relieved only by moving air. With removal of the interior sliding *fusuma* the house becomes an open pavilion, shelter expressed in elaborate sculptural terms by the roof.

Since primitive times, the floor in Japanese architecture has remained the common surface of activity—for sitting, living and sleeping. Wooden clogs, *geta*, worn outside are left at the doorstep upon entering the house; slipper socks with a heavy cloth sole, *tabi*, are worn inside so that no outside dirt or mud can be tracked onto the *tatami*. The floor of a Japanese house is especially notable. Whereas in most other civilizations it is associated with dirt, in Japan it has the intimate qualities of warmth and texture and is as important as any other surface plane in establishing the interior space. *Fusuma* and *shoji* are approximately the same height as the *tatami* are long, about six feet. This height, at the level of the grooved strip into which the top of *fusuma* and *shoji* fit, is emphasized by the *nageshi*, or molding, which continues this level around the room (plate 91); thus providing to one seated on the floor, a constant, stable frame of reference, no matter how large the room is. Decorative effects, the placement of objects, and, of course, construction of the garden are considered from the eye level of a person seated on *tatami*.

The usual household accessories, removed when not in use, include small, low tables, arm rests, an occasional folding screen and a portable brazier, *hibachi*, for warming the hands during winter. Sleeping quilts are stored out of sight during the day. Room functions are completely interchangeable and at any time a series of small rooms can, with removal of *fusuma*, become one large room. Lacking high or overbearing furniture, spaces are clear, defined only by textured planes whose materials manifest their own natural personality; *tatami* in lustrous tones of yellowish green, papered sliding screens, occasional solid walls of plaster, richly polished woods, and, when *shoji* are removed, a garden view. The *tokonoma*, found in almost every Japanese house, is the focal point of the interior, the place devoted solely and exclusively to the display of art—scroll paintings, flower arrangements, ceramic objects—changed with the seasons, the mood of the inhabitant, or any special occasion. The 18-mat *shoin* room of the Kojoin Kyakuden (plate 91) shows a very large *tokonoma* with a painted background, to its left the platformed area where the study desk is located (plate 92), and to its right the *tana* arrangement. All vertical divisions readily correspond either with *tatami* length or width. Less obvious at first is a kind of aesthetic tension in the interior: the ceiling floats, suspended from the heavy roof which in turn has no visible means of support. The columns end below the ceiling (or seem to), in deference to the desired effect, precluding the inherent logic of structure. Narrow strips of plaster conceal the continuation of the columns at the ceiling. Similar strips at the floor tend to isolate the walls and accentuate the visual activity of mat bindings and ceiling battens going in opposite directions. The animated quality of these interior relationships is entirely harmonious, their effect exercising an appeal in two and three dimensions similar to that which motivated the neo-plastic artists of the early twentieth century in the Western world.

Where a less definite division of space is required above the *fusuma*, solid plaster panels are replaced by woven or carved wood screens, *ramma*. Thus the effect of space from room to room, more or less continuous but stabilized by the heights of the sliding system, depends on the original intent of the builder with regard to room size and placement; the roof, shelter in abstract form, is admired for itself from the exterior. In this, feeling is more important to the Japanese than logic. An official edict was issued during the Nara Period to the effect that court nobles of the fifth rank and above build their houses with tile roofs and paint the columns red and the plaster white (they were obviously not doing so), while the Emperor himself could provide no better example than residence in a palace of plain wood with a *hinoki* bark roof. The formal propriety of Chinese models was always subject to the Japanese ideals of comfort, aesthetically and otherwise. The logical array of columns holding up a roof carries with it the idea of perspective, an architectural discipline of little interest to the Japanese. One exception, though not in domestic architecture, occurs in the Momoyama Palace Audience Hall, now located at the Nishi Honganji Temple in Kyoto.

Soon after the regency of Yoshimitsu, during the Ashikaga Shogunate, Japan entered a state of almost continual civil war. The name Ashikaga identifies the era mainly for chronological convenience rather than for actual rule. One powerful feudal lord, Oda Nobunaga, rose to campaign in the name of the Emperor and succeeded in restoring order in much of Japan with the help of Toyotomi Hideyoshi and Ieyasu Tokugawa, the former his general, the latter an ally, both of whom ruled in turn after Nobunaga. The modern history of Japan may be said to date from this time. Further securing the national stability instituted by Nobunaga, which had brought a good measure of prosperity with it, Hideyoshi began to build elaborate castles and mansions in which he conducted large-scale entertainments with the same energy that marked his rather sensational military achievements.

Unfortunately, little remains of Hideyoshi's constructions[13] although several portions of buildings are preserved, one of them the Audience Hall mentioned above (plate 94). It is a *shoin* room with a *jodan*, *tokonoma* in the center, and *tana* at the right, all of comparatively vast dimensions. Hideyoshi held court from the *jodan* centered between two rows of columns directly in front of the *tokonoma*. The perspective established is enforced—the last columns toward the *jodan* are more closely spaced with the express purpose of focusing attention on Hideyoshi. He really dominated the room, which in itself competed for attention, with its display of Hideyoshi's luxuriant tastes—elaborately carved and polychrome *ramma*, coffered ceiling panels with gold backgrounds, and mural-scale *fusuma* paintings of plum and pine trees and cranes. When the sliding screens at the other end are removed, the room looks out on a Noh drama stage across the court.

Hideyoshi's Momoyama Palace gave its name to the period in Japanese history which witnessed the intentional destruction of many powerful Buddhist temples (which by then were fortified, and with armed priests and paid mercenaries) as Nobunaga and Hideyoshi consolidated their political power. The Momoyama Period also saw the perfection of two architectural extremes: the tea house, tiny, rustic, peaceful in spirit; and the large castle complex, building interiors gorgeously decorated in the case of the Shoguns. The castle of a provincial clan chief was less elaborate, a means of permanent defense as well as a practical administrative center (plate 95). An improved defense against firearms and cannon introduced to Japan at this time, castles replaced the earthworks-stockade arrangement which characterized mobile warfare with foot soldiers, archers, and mounted swordsmen. Located on appropriate hill or mountain sites in or near district urban centers, they became focal points for the development of most major cities and towns in Japan. The city of Edo, now the capital of Tokyo, was first developed as a military administrative center, a sort of barrier-defense against powerful war lords in the north of Honshu. Typically, the local clan castle around which the modern city of Hikone has developed is based on the European defensive system of moats and escarpments ringed around a central keep. The main citadel at Hikone (plate 96) has the usual brightly whitewashed castle walls rising five stories, roofs and gables gradually diminishing in size, as functional from the standpoint of prestige (especially when viewed from a distance) as for actual defense. When they chose to work with stone the Japanese were excellent engineers, erecting massive yet sweepingly graceful ramparts of heavy granite blocks. Rampart walls were punctuated at key points by smaller donjons (plate 97). The lord of the territory lived in *shoin* rooms of the central keep or in a mansion close by, while extensive facilities for warriors and their equipment were made available behind the outer battlements. The arched shapes of large, naturally bent trees were put to ingenious structural use in Hikone's interior (plate 98); the walls were of heavy wood construction covered with plaster.

Large castle complexes, especially those of the Shoguns, had separate dwellings within the second defensive ring. Nijo Castle in Kyoto was originally built by Nobunaga for a protégé whom he later made Shogun. Except for rampart walls it now retains only the dwelling, or great *shoin* building, renovated by Shogun Ieyasu for use as a Kyoto headquarters. The real capital, with a tremendous castle complex, was in Edo, built with enforced contributions from clan lords all over Japan, whose power Ieyasu thereby controlled. This great mansion of Nijo (plates 99–103), part of the continuing demonstration of Shogunate power instituted in Kyoto by Nobunaga's original Nijo Castle, contains a richly decorated assortment of official apartments, audience and reception halls. Based on the type of mansion (plate 81) built earlier by Shogun Yoshimasa, in plan and outward appearance Nijo is a series of connected pavilions grouped in the typical Shoin echelon formation (plate 101). The exterior, composed of great roofs and precise geometrical façades, presents an effect not unlike that of the Imperial Palace complex. The reserved exterior contrasts with the interiors in which the full decorative magnificence of the Momoyama Period seems to have been released. Painting, carving, lacquer, and metal work combine in a symphony of polychrome and gold leaf. Mural-size paintings cover every *fusuma*, typical of the naturalistic art arrayed throughout the building, creating constantly changing vistas in every direction. Themes from nature are related within each room, the paintings on each set of panels carefully scaled in accordance with the space enclosed. There is no final climax except the explicit power of the Shogun for whom Nijo was made so that he could slide nature back to reveal architecture (plate 102). Held within bounds at Nijo, the ostentation of Momoyama times erupted into a final decadent display at Nikko, where the Tokugawa Shoguns, Ieyasu and Iemitsu, created a pair of mausolea for themselves. In a strangely mixed atmosphere of Buddhism and Shinto, combined to support deification of the two Shoguns, a series of temples, shrines, pagodas, libraries, bell and drum towers, and gates, arranged in compounds or individually, ascends a series of hillside terraces to the mausolea themselves. Exemplified by the Yomeimon Gate (plate 104), the structures exhibit the most elaborate coloring, carving, metalwork, sculpture, gilding—every sort of decorative effect known. This marvelous cacophony is, however, embraced by a forest of Cryptomeria trees, which, just beyond the precincts of the mausolea, restores the prevalence of nature (plate 105).

The mainstream of Japanese architecture was fed by traditions of structure, plan, materials, and a modular system that led to the development of the sort of domestic architecture described in the Kojoin Kyakuden (plates 87–93). The art of external environment, the garden, was no less a matter for aesthetic concern to the Japanese. Site as well as the seasonal variety of nature was taken into account in producing the desired surroundings and visual effects.

The particularly Japanese concept of gardens stems from a variety of sources. Among these are the original open clearing for Shinto ceremonials and early moated palaces or dwellings, which may have given rise to artificial pond islands. Most important, however, were the Korean craftsmen who, coming with cultural importations during the Nara Period, created "mountain shapes" for landscape gardens. Early poems mention the beauty of Nara gardens. These, as well as a park constructed in the Imperial Palace compound of Heian times, were probably based on T'ang Dynasty and earlier Chinese use of artificial parks with lakes in which pond islands represented the dwelling places of mythological personages. The original Heian Period Shinden mansion gardens, used for boating and strolling, had special religious significance as symbolic of Amida Buddha's paradise. At the same time Japanese preference began to exert itself with representations of the native landscape, a development that continued into the fifteenth century, by which time Zen Buddhism had imparted a new subjective quality to garden making. An aesthetic high point was reached within the next two hundred years during which three basic types of gardens may be distinguished: the pond gardens, the dry landscape garden in which water was implied or symbolized, and the flat garden, characteristic of Zen Buddhist temples. Whether conceived in a naturalistic, symbolic, or philosophical sense, gardens were always a consciously careful blend of trees, rocks, shrubs, moss, and sand.

Originally containing an Amida Hall, which seems to account for the pond garden of its lower level, Saihoji Temple later became a Zen establishment whose priest, Muso Kokushi, constructed the earliest remaining examples of "dry cascades" on the upper slopes of the garden (plate 106). Whether or not his garden was a physical application in Zen, Muso (the foremost Zen priest of the time, holding the respect of the ruling Shogun) had obviously attempted a more symbolically significant expression, beyond the mere representation or enhancement of certain qualities of natural landscape. Supposed to have been influenced by the Saihoji Temple Garden, Yoshimasa's Higashiyamaden (East Mountain Villa) (plate 81) has little left of its extensive series of buildings and shows a greatly reduced pond, too small for the boating parties which are known to have taken place there (plate 107). Unlike its spiritual predecessor, the Kinkaku (plate 79), it was given a site at the foot of the mountains bordering Kyoto on the east, with the specific intention of borrowing the mountain's scenery. In the seventeenth century several unusual additions occurred in this garden when it was converted into a temple known as the Jishoji. These include two piles of weather-stiffened white sand: one cone shaped, six feet high and sixteen feet in diameter across its base, known as Kogetsudai, or Moon Facing Mound; the other a flat curved terrace about two feet high, called Ginshanada, or Silver Sand Sea (plate 109). These forms seem to have been derived from the use of a sand-strewn rectangular space or court for ceremonial purposes (seen at other Buddhist temples, plate 108) with piles of sand kept to one side for replacement. The flat sand terrace at Jishoji is unique; for although it seems to represent the sea, its real purpose is a matter of conjecture.

At the Samboin Temple, south of Kyoto, one of the most elaborately concentrated of all pond gardens owes its existence to the irrepressible Hideyoshi who enlarged it at the end of the sixteenth century and made it the scene for cherry-blossom-viewing festivals. One portion was made into a flat sand garden with circles of moss, some joined to form a gourd shape (plate 110), in what seems to be a specific allusion to Hideyoshi's battle standard from which hung a set of bottle-shaped gourds. The pond garden nearby (plate 111), small and with a closed vista, is nevertheless richly endowed with hundreds of fine rocks, some brought from great distances, many requisitioned from other gardens.[14] Notable for its absence of rocks, the upper garden of Shugakuin Palace is the finest of three gardens completed in the middle of the seventeenth century as part of the estate for a retired Emperor. Covering an area of about fifty acres, the upper garden, really a park, is broadly conceived and executed; its wooded hills, clipped hedges, smooth sod banks, and quiet lake blend with the distant landscape, achieving in effect the pastoral character of an English park (plate 112).

Considered by the Japanese to be one of the greatest master-pieces of garden art, the Daisenin Garden is indirectly related to Sung landscape painting—a thirteenth-century development of China's highest civilization which inspired Japanese painters of the Muromachi Period two hundred years later. Just as the Japanese black-and-white school of painting achieved its own distinct quality to equal the genius of the original Sung masters, so the rocks of the Daisenin capture by plastic means what had been expressed in the angular ink brushwork of landscape paintings by Shubun and Sesshu. The Daisenin (plates 113–115), located in the Daitokuji Temple at Kyoto, was created in 1509. Laid out in the shape of a carpenter's square, it is a small garden with rocks carefully selected to represent a mountain cascade and stream, with islands, bridges, and a boat. (The stream of sand disappears under an arched corridor bridge at the other end.) Set against a white plaster wall and viewed from the veranda of the priest's residence, the garden provides a vivid atmosphere for associative meditation.

Among the gardens of Kyoto's Zen temples, that of Ryoanji

(plates 116–118) is the most remarkable. Built toward the end of the fifteenth century, it was completely different from all the gardens that preceded it. Behind the monastery walls, in a flat rectangular area approximately the size of a tennis court, fifteen stones in groups of two, three, and five are set into the earth, which is covered with a bed of coarse white sand. Small areas of moss now surround some of the stones, but these probably were not originally intended.

Speculative interpretations of Ryoanji range from the trigonometric through the esoteric to the occult; its real "meaning" is simply not known. After feeling its impact as a completely new visual experience consisting simply of rocks, sand, and space, the Western observer becomes aware of certain relationships, between the individual stones and their groups, between the groups themselves, and finally within the entire spatial environment. The ultimate significance, however, lies deep within Zen, suggested by the powerful sensory impression evoked, but elusive, like the one stone in Ryoanji which can never be seen from any position on the viewing platform.

The force of Ryoanji demonstrates a kind of cosmic quality that precludes even the use of trees and growing things; but more immediately understandable to the Japanese is the transient quality of his own domestically scaled garden—basically a matter of contemplation rather than the scene for human activity—molded by the more simple universal truths of rain, sunlight, snow, and the seasons.

Nurtured by the Ashikaga Shoguns, the organized precepts of Zen Buddhism which arrived in Japan during the thirteenth century differed considerably from the mainstream of Buddhist thought that originally entered Japan in the sixth century. Possessed of no written scriptures, its superlogical doctrines difficult to grasp, and final enlightenment within it attainable by very few, Zen nevertheless presented tenets understandable enough to form a practical discipline of art. Simplicity, restraint, and the elimination of the insignificant were among the obvious requirements of Zen in life, art, and Chanoyu—the tea ceremony. Tea drinking, originally from China, was first practiced by Zen monks to keep awake during meditation in their study halls. Later it became an active part of Zen rituals honoring Bodhidharma, their first patriarch. Developing from this, the tea ceremony at its best came to be a gathering of friends in an isolated atmosphere to partake of tea and discuss the artistic merit of certain objects—a scroll painting or an example of calligraphy hanging in the *tokonoma*, perhaps the flower arrangement below it, or often the utensils of the tea service.

The first tea ceremonies took place under the patronage of Shogun Yoshimasa in the Togudo's four-and-one-half-mat tea room (plate 83) at Higashiyamaden where he instituted a cultural form unique to Japan—a place reserved solely and specifically for the active appreciation of art. The tea ceremony grew in popularity, giving rise to a set of tea masters, for the most part Zen monks and scholars who, applying the characteristic standards of Teaism—an allusive, restrained sort of aestheticism—exercised functions of creative criticism in various art fields: painting, ceramics, flower arranging, and calligraphy, as well as architecture for Tea. They also established a specific discipline for behavior during the tea ceremony. The cult embraced a complete cultural range, appealing at one extreme to the Shogun, who could discuss with a sympathetic critic his latest artistic acquisitions from the continent, and at the other to the ordinary *samurai*, who could enjoy a cup of tea in a peacefully educational atmosphere (a special sword rack was provided at the entrance). Participation in a tea ceremony became akin to possession of a *shoin* desk during the earlier Kamakura Period.

The greatest tea master of all, Sen-no-Rikyu (1521–91), was the first to build a separate *chashitsu*, or tea house, which was a distinct physical entity instead of a specially decorated room within the house. Since then, the *chashitsu*, ideally separated from the house, has been approached through a small garden, called *roji* (Dewy Path), the first step in breaking connection with the outer world (plate 120). The tea house (plate 119) is a small thatch-roofed structure with plain plaster walls whose several shoji-covered openings placed at different heights admit a soft, diffuse light. The interior ranges in size from the generally standard four-and-one-half mats down to two mats—large enough to accommodate five kneeling guests. Set above a stepping stone, the small "kneeling-in" entrance, about two and one half feet square, is intended to inculcate humility in all who enter. In subtle affinity with a process in which the spirit alone is to prevail, the *chashitsu* is completely bare, materials are plain and undecorated, color and texture the natural result of materials used. Absent are balance and symmetry, with their resulting sense of completeness which, according to Chanoyu, inhibits the imagination and allows for no further growth. Suggestive presences and tacit absences are translated into an atmosphere of austere tranquility (plate 121), the felicitous setting for the Zen "art of being in the world".

Taian (Expecting Place), a tiny two-mat tea house (plates 122–124) attached to the Myokian Temple near Kyoto, was built in 1582 by Rikyu (who was also a garden maker and an expert flower arranger, as well as an all-round connoisseur) for Hideyoshi, under whose patronage Teaism attained its highest development. (A frequent guest of the aesthetic mentor in the Taian, Hideyoshi may be recalled as presiding over his vassals in the 4,000-square-foot Audience Hall of the contemporary Momoyama Castle.) The Taian's two-mat floor has one corner cut out for the hearth over which the tea kettle was heated. The *tokonoma* is the size of a half mat. Construction and materials are of the utmost simplicity, the wood partly smooth, retaining a delicate rustic feeling; the plaster revealing the natural sand and straw of which it was made—the fundamental quality of things expressed.

The Bosen (Final Attainment) Tea Room was built in 1612 by Kobori Enshu, the leading tea master of the seventeenth century, who was also a poet and painter, and particularly famous as a garden maker. Really Enshu's study, the Bosen (plates 125–127) is a twelve-mat room with a double, stepped veranda overlooking the garden. In this design Enshu demonstrated the inventive qualities which made him a leader of taste in many artistic fields. Disregarding convention, he oriented the room toward the west and devised a most unusual suspended *shoji* which shielded the interior from heat and glare while permitting a view of the garden from beneath it (plate 126). A division of the interior space is implied by the axial disposition of the mats which differentiate the rear three-mat tea-ceremony space from the main nine-mat area (plate 127). This subtle sort of usage is but one aspect of the interior whose seemingly simple expression was thoughtfully calculated by Enshu. Its "classic" feeling contrasts with Rikyu's Taian which, using the same materials—wood, plaster, and matting—is rustic and poetical. Thus, as the spirit of tea-house architecture found its way into the vocabulary of domestic building, the Sukiya (tea house) style came to characterize the *shoin* building whose aesthetic climate now began to exhibit a conscious rustic quality.

42

The Sukiya style figures prominently in the Katsura Imperial Palace (plates 128–147), originally a princely estate built during the early seventeenth century. This complex of buildings summarizes the prevailing ideals of architecture and garden art at the peak of their artistic development. Located in the southwest suburbs of Kyoto on the bank of the Katsura River, which supplies water for its ponds and streams, the estate covers an area of about sixteen acres. It was given to Toshihito, the younger brother of the current Emperor, by Hideyoshi in 1590. Prince Toshihito, whose aesthetic tastes were manifest in literature, especially poetry, was the dominant personality in the creation of Katsura. He developed the estate until his death in 1629. During the next few years it was completed in substantially its present form by his son, Prince Toshitada, who built an addition to the main section, two more tea pavilions, and much of the garden's stonework.

Bamboo fences and high bamboo hedges bound the estate, enclosing it completely. Set into the landscape which has been expressly created around them, the main buildings of Katsura consist of three attached structures: Ko-shoin, Chu-shoin, and Shin-shoin—Old, Middle, and New Halls, respectively. In plan they form the typical Shoin style of buildings in echelon, roofs intersecting, interior spaces under them freely organized. The high wooden posts supporting the Chu-shoin and Shin-shoin were necessary to maintain the same floor level throughout, despite the sloping site. Façades are unified by the modular system maintained but slightly varied in the elegant *shoji* proportions, and by the stepped rhythm of the veranda-supporting posts and the eave lines of the roofs. Emphasizing their indigenous character, the Irimoya style roofs are not concave but convex—a last vestige of "official" architecture which here makes its departure, having given way to the tradition first manifest at Ise, continued in innumerable examples of domestic and farm-house architecture throughout Japan, and finally promoted by Teaism. Open spaces surrounding the Shoin façades allow them to be seen clearly. Access to the garden is possible at the level of the Ko-shoin; from its covered veranda one steps down onto pathways (Plate 131) on either side of the Moon Viewing Platform. Extending forward from the Ko-shoin veranda, and typical of a poetic association translated physically, the Moon Viewing Platform recalls an ancient legend recommending the area southwest of Kyoto, where Katsura is located, as an especially favorable place for viewing the moon. The Platform is a simple bamboo terrace facing the spot where the moon rises, commanding the best view of the lake (plate 132).

Although they are harmoniously related, the interiors of Katsura differ. The original Ko-shoin and Chu-shoin suites are simpler in effect than the Shin-shoin, built later on the occasion of an Imperial visit, which shows an elaborate set of *tana* shelves, a decorative window alcove above the *shoin* desk, and a dropped ceiling above the *jodan* platform, the whole combining to give a more official quality to this chief room of the Shin-shoin (plates 136, 137). The *fusuma* motif of an all-over pattern of silver leaves carries continuity from the earlier Ko-shoin and Chu-shoin, which are similarly decorated but generally more relaxed in feeling, their environment expressive of a kind of intellectual ease best demonstrated in the three-mat Musical Instruments Room of the Chu-shoin (plate 135).

Both Princes responsible for Katsura were devotees of the tea ceremony, as were all the literati of the times; and as a result the Palace has four tea pavilions about its grounds, one for each season of the year. These pavilions together with their garden environment seem to embody the delicacy and sophistication of certain pastoral poems of the *Kokinshu*, an anthology of short verses of the Heian Period. The *Kokinshu* was one of Prince Toshihito's main scholarly concerns, as was the *Tale of Genji*, a Heian romance much of whose action took place in mansions about the Katsura area.

The tea pavilion devoted to the spring season, Shokintei (Arbor of Soughing Pines), is placed on a promontory in the lake across from the Shoin buildings (plate 141). As one approaches it on foot, one passes some of Katsura's remarkable stone work. Each of the stones in the Palace grounds—from the smallest pebbles to the single massive slab bridging a stream—was painstakingly placed as part of the over-all design which ranges from the most subtle array of textured stepping stones to a miniature granite wilderness (plates 139–142).

More an example of fashionable aestheticism than a setting for the tea ceremony, the Shokintei is constructed like a cottage and contains several rooms, including a kitchen, in addition to the tea-ceremony room. It generally manifests picturesque qualities in intended contrast to the austere Shoin façades; the *tokonoma* and *fusuma* of its main room are decorated with a checkered pattern whose blue squares can be seen from the Shoin across the pond (plate 143).

Perhaps the most deliberate aesthetic effects at Katsura are found in the tea room of the Shokintei. The elements of its exterior façade (plate 145) are bamboo lath windows, textured plaster, and smoothed wooden posts—the simplest of materials, but combined into a most sophisticated architectural commentary. Exterior as well as interior (plate 144) approach that state of refinement where architecture becomes too ingeniously articulate. The art which had been embodied in the tea ceremony was now being surpassed by its own environment (partially as a means of release from the exaggerated formalism of the tea ritual itself[15]). Sukiya style becomes excessive when its elements tend to occupy a room rather than create its atmosphere. The essential reality is the space of a room waiting, as it were, to fulfill its function as a background for human activity—the evident contrast between the "activity" of Shokintei's tea room and the real sense of detachment in Rikyu's Taian or Enshu's Bosen.

Among the other tea pavilions at Katsura is the Shoiken (plate 146), which takes the form of a small farm house from which can be seen neighboring rice paddies outside this corner of the grounds. From earliest times farm houses have carried an unvarying native tradition of architecture throughout rural Japan, building styles changing slightly from one prefecture to another but always characterized by neatness and an innate sense of proportion combined with primitive strength. The rustic dignity of their thatch roofs was sought to complement the tea ceremony (plate 119). Modeled after the farm house style of the Kyoto district, the roof of the Shoiken shelters the largest tea pavilion at Katsura. Under the eaves is an arrangement of large rough stones, less refined than others at Katsura, but consistent with a "broader" effect that might conceivably result if a farmer were to choose rocks for his own garden (plate 147).

One example of the possibilities inherent in Sukiya techniques shows architecture taken beyond a sense of detachment—almost to the point of removal. Contemporary with Katsura, the Yoko-kan, a seventeenth-century villa in Fukui city, displays an unusual refinement of structure (plates 148–150). In effect balancing the shingle roofs, structure is not much more than an allusion on the interior, the idea of support seemingly concentrated outside the building proper, in posts holding up the overhanging eaves. So tentative is the enclosure of space that what little there is of the architecture seems to dissolve in the reflection of light from the lake (plate 149).

45

Katsura and the Yokokan give unparalleled demonstrations of architectural taste conforming with nature, maintaining felicitous control, extracting effects of the most delicate sensibility—stopping short of the point where the relationship between aesthetics and function becomes blurred and disturbing.

However "aesthetic-becoming" the potentialities of Sukiya style, it was basically a means of intensifying the underlying commitment of the Japanese to nature. The elements of its vocabulary are widespread in Japanese domestic architecture of the last four hundred years, not always with the intellectual refinement of a Katsura or Yokokan, but evident in ordinary dwellings through touches of rustic simplicity; for example, a *tokonoma* post in its natural state or a *shoji*-covered wall opening exposing the bamboo lath in which a growing vine seems to be entangled. These were variants on the basic theme of the Japanese dwelling to which nature's self-creating process gave an indefinable spiritual quality. If Shinto and Zen Buddhism are to be called religions, then a man's house in Japan was not his castle; it resembled rather his church.

# POSTSCRIPT

Modern architecture in Japan dates from about the end of the First World War. It followed a period of eclectic architecture in Gothic and Renaissance styles, primarily under European influence, which lasted from the time Japan officially ended its isolation in 1868 to about 1912. The new design tradition, signaled with the building of Frank Lloyd Wright's Imperial Hotel, later developed along the lines of the Bauhaus movement and the International Style, formulated by men like Walter Gropius, Mies van der Rohe, and especially Le Corbusier, with whom several important Japanese architects have studied. The creative effort of this first group of Japanese architects served to inspire a second generation of architects, all of whom are now fully attuned to industrially derived techniques, to their own cultural heritage, and to a new social, environmental awareness. Against this background many original, energetic Japanese designers are achieving brilliant results. However, aspects of their art, consciously or otherwise, relate to traditional forms.

Sutemi Horiguchi, of the first generation of architects, has gone through several phases, his early work showing an interest in the rationale of the Bauhaus which he visited in the 1920's. In the Okada House garden of 1934 (plate 151) he successfully unified traditional garden elements with clearly defined horizontal planes in a precise contemporary design. The fusion here of past and present is truly masterful.

One of the more dramatic examples of modern Japanese architecture is Junzo Sakakura's Museum of Modern Art at Kamakura—a blend of new industrial materials with native volcanic stone (plate 152). Its fully enclosed exhibition floor, containing skylighted galleries, is raised above the ground on thin steel columns and itself encloses an open court. The lower rooms, set under the overhang, are constructed of natural stone while the upper façades consist of light asbestos panels in an ashlar pattern. Among the most effective details in the carefully integrated sequences of space and volume are the steel posts resting on stone footings in the pond (in turn resting on concrete footings)—a translation of the classic system of Japanese foundations into modern construction (plate 153).

A last example is a proposed city plan for Tokyo where phenomenal growth has brought about problems whose monumentality is exceeded only by their rate of increase. This plan, developed by a team of architects under the direction of Kenzo Tange, one of Japan's foremost architects, calls for linear expansion of the city across Tokyo Bay with a great central axis of office buildings, mercantile facilities, and government offices. Residential areas would be located between perpendicular systems of streets extending out from the central axis (plate 154). Residential blocks take the form of concave pairs of terraced concrete levels sweeping down to the bay from great heights, assymetrically grouped and, in this well-studied, visionary solution reminiscent (if one may take a last backward look), of so many farm houses in a rural village or even a set of Shoin style roofs—under the influence of traditions that seem to exercise themselves.

These examples, taken out of context, cannot begin to suggest the dynamic building activity—industrial, commercial, domestic, and public—now taking place throughout Japan. They do underline some of the problems presented to architects who are faced with an aesthetic based on deeply rooted cultural traditions but who must now conceive of design in the fully industrial terms of modern Japan.

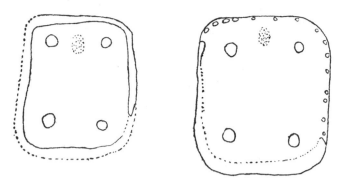

*1. Jomon Pit-Dwelling, prehistoric period. Site remains.*

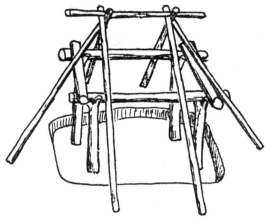

*2a. Jomon Pit-Dwelling. Structural framework.*

*2b. Jomon Pit-Dwelling. Reconstructed appearance.*

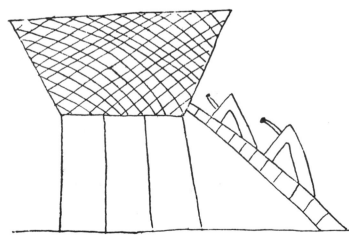

*3a. Yayoi High-Floor Dwelling,
first to fifth centuries A.D.*

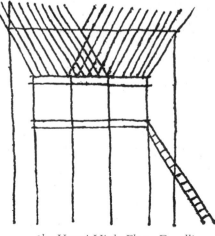

*3b. Yayoi High-Floor Dwelling.
Schematic representation.*

*a. High-Floor dwelling with balcony.*        *b. High-floor dwelling.*

*c. Ground-level house.*        *d. Pit-dwelling.*

**4.** *Dwellings shown on bronze mirror, fifth century.*

*5a. Haniwa House, ca. fifth century.*        *5b. Haniwa House, ca. fifth century.*

6. *Tomb of Emperor Nintoku near Osaka, middle of the fifth century.*

7. *Ise Naiku (Inner Shrine), Ise Prefecture, third century. Air view showing the newly built (1953) Shrine on the left.*

8. *Ise Naiku. Torii at outermost fence.*

9. *Ise Naiku. Drawing made about 1890.*

10. *Ise Naiku. Shoden (Main Sanctuary). Drawing made about 1890.*

11. *Ise Naiku. Shoden.*

12. *Ise Naiku. The small structure on the right protects the place over which the Sacred Mirror will be placed in the next rebuilding.*

13. Ise Naiku. Honden (Treasure House).

*14. Ise Naiku. Rear view of Shoden.*

*15. Ise Naiku. Shoden plan and elevations.*

*16. Shimmeigu Shrine, Nagano Prefecture.*
*Shimmei Shrine building style.*

17. *Izumo Shrine, Izumo Prefecture, ca. first century.*

18. *High-Floor Dwelling, ca. second to fifth centuries.*

19. *Izumo Shrine. Plan and elevations.*

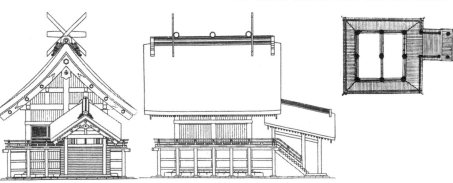

20. *Kasuga Shrine style. Plan and elevations.*

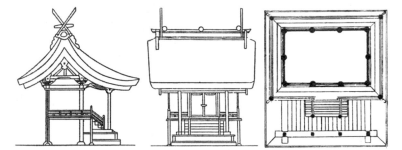

21. *Nagare Shrine style.* Plan and elevations.

22. *Nachi Shrine, Wakayama Prefecture. Nagare style.*

*23. Horyuji Temple Compound, Nara, end of the seventh century.*

*24. Horyuji Kondo (Main Hall).*

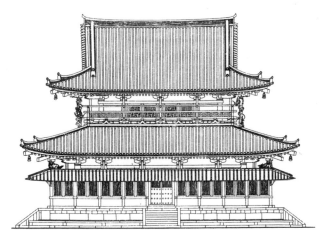

*25. Horyuji Kondo. Elevation drawing.*

26. *Horyuji Gojunoto (Pagoda).*

27. *Horyuji Chumon (Middle Gate).*

28. *Todaiji Temple Hokkedo, Nara, early eighth century.*

29. *Todaiji Hokkedo. Interior ceiling detail.*

30. *Todaiji Hokkedo. Exterior showing bracketing.*

31. *Toshodaiji Temple Kondo (Main Hall), Nara, eighth century.*

32. *Toshodaiji Kondo. Colonnade.*

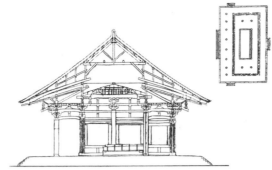

*33. Toshodaiji Kondo. Section and plan.*

*34. Toshodaiji Kondo. Interior.*

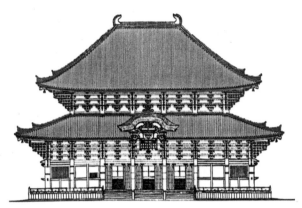

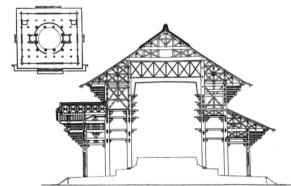

35. *Todaiji Daibutsuden. Front elevation.*

36. *Todaiji Daibutsuden. Plan and section.*

37. *Todaiji Daibutsuden. Exterior bracketing detail.*

38. *Todaiji Daibutsuden. Interior.*

*39. Todaiji Daibutsuden. Detail from Shigi-san engi, a twelfth-century scroll painting.*

*40. Todaiji Temple Daibutsuden (Buddha Hall), Nara, founded in 745. The largest wooden building in the world under one roof.*

41. *Todaiji Daibutsuden. The Great Buddha.*

42. *Todaiji* **Temple** *Shosoin (Imperial Repository), Nara, 745. End view.*

43. *Todaiji Shosoin.*

44. *Toshodaiji Temple Keizo (Treasure Houses), Nara, eighth century.*

45. *Muroji Temple Kondo (Main Hall)*, **Nara Prefecture**, tenth to twelfth centuries.

46. *Muroji Pagoda. Section and plan.*                    47. *Muroji Pagoda.*

48. *Sambutsuji Temple, Tottori Prefecture, ca. twelfth century.*

49. *Kongosanmaiin Tahoto (Pagoda), Wakayama Prefecture, ca. thirteenth century.*

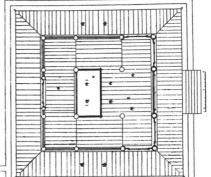

*51. Shiramizu Amidado. Plan.*

*50. Shiramizu Amidado (Amida Buddha Hall), Fukushima Prefecture, twelfth century.*

*52. Shiramizu Amidado. Interior.*

53. *Byodoin Temple Hoodo (Phoenix Hall), Uji near Kyoto, 1053. Heian Period villa converted into an Amida Hall.*

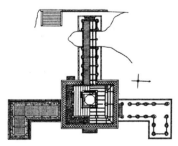

54. *Byodoin Hoodo. Plan.*

55. *Byodoin Hoodo. Interior detail.*

56. *Byodoin Hoodo. Interior showing the Amida Buddha.*

57. *Engakuji Shariden (Reliquary Hall), Kanagawa Prefecture, 1298.*

58. *Engakuji Shariden. Elevation.*

59. *Engakuji Shariden. Section.*

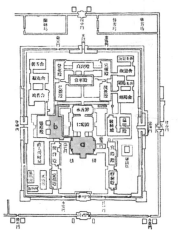

60. *Imperial Palace Buildings.*
   *Plan: a) Shishinden; b) Seiryoden.*

62. *Imperial Palace, Kyoto. Air view.*

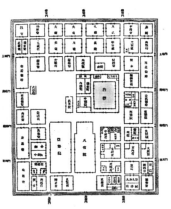

61. *Imperial Compound, Kyoto. Imperial Palace buildings in the shaded area.*

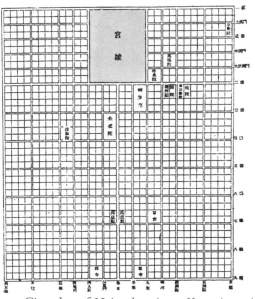

63. *City plan of Heian-kyo (now Kyoto), capital of Japan from 793 to 1869. Shaded area is the Imperial Compound.*

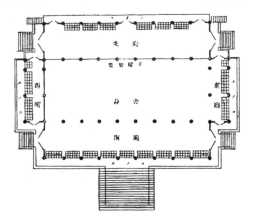

64. *Imperial Palace. Shishinden. Plan.*

65. *Imperial Palace. Shishinden, (Front Hall of Audience).*

*66. Imperial Palace. Shishinden. Interior.*

67. *Imperial Palace. Seiryoden (Serene and Cool Hall). The Emperor's dwelling.*

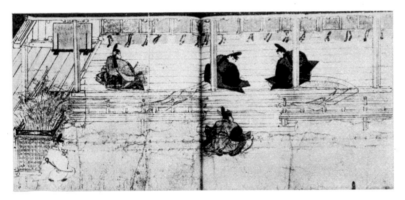

68. *Imperial Palace. Scene before the Seiryoden, from Shigi-san engi, a twelfth-century scroll painting.*

69. *Imperial Palace. Seiryoden. Interior.*

70. *Imperial Palace. Seiryoden. Interior showing the Sekkaidan, Imperial ritual space.*

71. *Imperial Palace. Seiryoden. Plan.*

72. *Imperial Palace. Corridor connecting the Shishinden and Seiryoden.*

73. *Shinden style dwelling, ninth to twelfth centuries.*

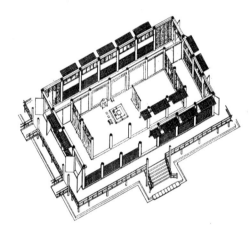

74. *Moya (main room) of Shinden dwelling.*

75. *Fujiwara clan Shinden, Tosanjoden, Heian Period. Plan.*

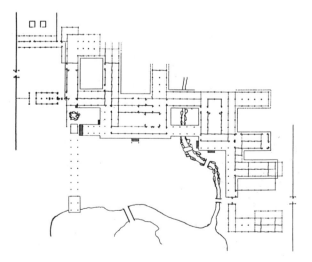

76. *High-ranking Shinden interior, from Kasuga Gongen Reikenki, a fourteenth-century scroll painting.*

77. *Shinden interior of a lesser noble, from Ishiyamadera engi, a fourteenth-century scroll painting.*

78. *Warrior's house of the thirteenth century from Ippen Hijiri e.*

79. *Kinkaku (Golden Pavilion), Kyoto, end of the fourteenth century.*

80. *Ginkaku (Silver Pavilion), Kyoto, 1489.*

81. *Reconstruction of Higashiyamaden, villa of the Shogun Yoshimasa. (Ginkaku at far left, Togudo at far right.)*

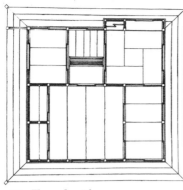

82. Togudo. Plan.

83. Togudo. Interior showing tana and shoin.

84. Togudo. Shoin alcove from exterior.

85. Togudo, Kyoto, 1486. Exterior.

86. Priest's house of the fourteenth century showing shoin desk, from Ishiyamadera engi.

87. *Kojoin Kyakuden, Otsu, 1600. Veranda.*

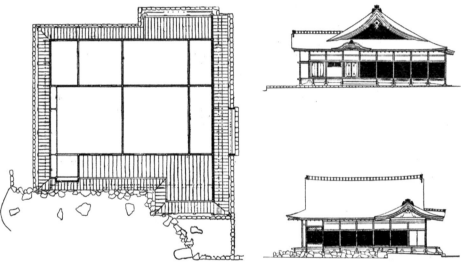

88. *Kojoin Kyakuden. Plan.*

89. *Kojoin Kyakuden. Elevations.*

90. *Kojoin Kyakuden. Exterior.*

*91. Kojoin Kyakuden. Interior, principal room.*

*92. Kojoin Kyakuden. Interior, shoin desk alcove.*

*93. Kojoin Kyakuden. Interior.*

*94. Audience Hall, Momoyama Castle, ca. 1600. Now at Nishi Honganji Temple, Kyoto.*

*95. Matsumoto Castle, Matsumoto, 1582.*

*96. Hikone Castle, Hikone, seventeenth century. Exterior.*

*97 Hikone Castle.*
*Drawbridge entrance.*

*98. Hikone Castle. Donjon interior.*

*99. Nijo Castle, Kyoto. Shoin Mansion, early seventeenth century.*

*100. Nijo Shoin. Exterior.*

*101. Nijo Shoin. Plan.*

*102. Nijo Shoin. Interior.*

*103. Nijo Shoin. Interior.*

104. *Yomeimon Gate, Mausoleum of Shogun Ieyasu, Nikko, early seventeenth century.*

105. *Cryptomeria trees, Nikko.*

*106. Saihoji Temple Garden, Kyoto, 1339. Dry cascade.*

*107. Jishoji (Ginkaku) Temple Garden, Kyoto, seventeenth century.*

*108. Daitokuji Temple Hojo Garden, Kyoto, sixteenth century.*

*109. Jishoji Garden. "Moon Facing Mound" and "Silver Sand Sea."*

*110. Samboin Temple Garden, south of Kyoto, ca. 1600. Sand garden.*

*111. Samboin Garden. Pond garden.*

*112. Shugakuin Palace Garden, Kyoto, ca. 1665. Upper garden.*

113. *Daisenin Garden. Detail.*

114. *Daisenin Garden.*
     *View from the priest's dwelling.*   115. *Daitokuji Temple Daisenin Garden, Kyoto, 1509.*

*116. Ryoanji Garden. Detail.*

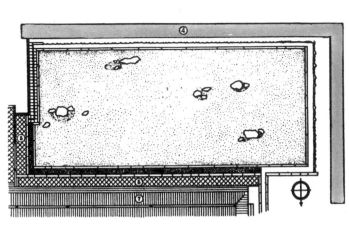

*117. Ryoanji Garden. Plan.*

*118. Ryoanji Temple Garden, near Kyoto, ca. 1500.*

*119. Tea House exterior. (Matsushita-an Tea House, Kyoto).*

*120. Roji Garden. (Suian Tea House, Kyoto).*

*121. Tea House interior. (Kokyuan Tea House, Kyoto).*

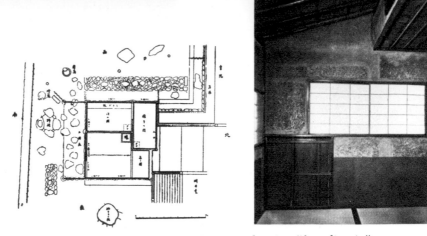

122. Taian Tea House. Plan.    123. Taian Tea House. Interior showing "kneeling-in" entrance.

124. Taian Tea House, Kyoto, 1582.

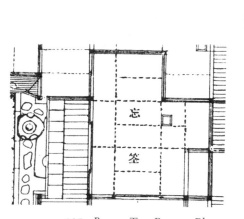

125. *Bosen Tea Room. Plan.*

126. *Bosen Tea Room. Detail showing suspended shoji.*

127. *Bosen Tea Room, Kyoto, 1612.*

*128. Katsura Imperial Palace, Kyoto, 1590–1636.*

*129. Katsura Palace. Shoin buildings.*

130. *Katsura Palace. Shoin buildings. The Ko-shoin (Old Shoin) is at the right, behind it to the left are the Chu-shoin (Middle) and the Shin-shoin (New).*

131. *Katsura Palace. Ko-shoin entrance.*

132. Katsura Palace. Moon Viewing Platform.

133. Katsura Palace. Chu-shoin façade.

*134. Katsura Palace. Ko-shoin interior.*

*135. Katsura Palace. Musical Instruments Room.*

*136. Katsura Palace.* Jodan *area in the* Shin-shoin *showing* tana *shelves and* shoin *desk.*

*137. Katsura Palace.* Shin-shoin.

*138. Katsura Palace. View from the Ko-shoin.*

139. Katsura Palace. Garden entrance from the outer grounds.

140. Katsura Palace. Garden path.

*141. Katsura Palace. View toward Shokintei Tea Pavilion.*

*142. Katsura Palace. Garden path.*

143. Katsura Palace.
Shokintei Tea Pavilion interior.

144. Katsura Palace. Shokintei Tea Room interior.

145. Katsura Palace. Exterior façade of the Shokintei Tea Room.

146. *Katsura Palace. Shoiken Tea Pavilion.*

147. *Katsura Palace. Under the eaves of the Shoiken.*

*148. Yokokan Pavilion, Fukui, seventeenth century.*

*149. Yokokan. Interior.*

*150. Yokokan. Exterior.*

*151. Sutemi Horiguchi, Garden for Okada House, Tokyo, 1934.*

*152. Junzo Sakakura, Kamakura Museum of Modern Art, Kamakura, 1951.*

*153. Kamakura Museum of Modern Art. Detail.*

*154. Kenzo Tange, City Plan for Tokyo, 1960.*

# NOTES

1. All dates are henceforth A.D. in both text and photo captions unless otherwise indicated. Divisions into architectural periods, according to the system of Professor Jiro Murata of Kyoto University, are found in the Chronology on page 117 These dates, varying with individual interpretation, are for general use only. For instance, "Early Nara" (645–707) is obviously a misnomer, referring to the time just before the capital of Nara was founded, but is included within the Nara Period in the stylistic sense. The same is true of the Heian Period which followed.

2. Among these were the Sacred Mirror, Sword, and Jewel, at first in the possession of the Emperor, later placed in shrines. The Mirror at the Ise Shrine is the "august spirit-substitute" for the Sun Goddess Amaterasu, the first child of the original creation myth deities. The attribution of divine ancestry to the Imperial clan included a transference of their physical possessions of the highest status—early bronze armor, swords, mirrors, as well as jade, agate, and crystal jewelry—into a means of symbolic authority.

3. Despite the immense knowledge of ancient Japan which could be gained from investigation of the Imperial tombs, past Emperors are allowed a continuing state of heavenly rest by the Japanese, although their passage from one state of religious belief into another had its fervent moments. This example of "human" continuity over a remarkable length of time in the East may be compared with the state of archaeological anticipation in the West that greeted the discovery of a pagan tomb, in Egypt or Greece, whose occupant, after his intimate belongings had been taken from him, was measured, unwrapped, photographed, displayed, and published, having all the while been the subject of morbid arguments as to final possession. The analytical spirit has its interesting aspects.

4. Certain creation myths of Oceania (in addition to architectural systems) bear strong resemblances to those of the Japanese. Izanagi and Izanami, the first recognized deities, are said to have circled around the "august central pillar,"

which signified a connection between heaven and earth, as part of the ceremonies leading to their marriage, the birth first of the islands of Japan and then of their daughter, the Sun Goddess (*Cf.* note 2). Dedicated to the nephew of the Sun Goddess, Izumo Shrine is located, however, in an area originally populated, according to legend and artifacts discovered there, by Mongol stock coming via Korea. Specific proofs of Japanese racial origin are yet to be presented.

5. The *torii*, found at the entrance to every Shinto shrine, is usually made of two posts set into the ground with a top crosspiece extending past the posts and a second crosspiece just below the top connecting the posts. Its derivation is again conjectural, hinted at by ancient usages: a straw rope stretched between two trees or posts marking a sanctified Shinto site, the rope in time being replaced by a log bound to two trees or posts, later refined to become a separate "gateway."

6. Pagodas are adaptations of the hemispherical brick or stone mounds of India called *stupas*, originally erected to preserve the relics of Gautama Buddha. This form later developed into a raised stone structure in India and into towers in the other Oriental countries which adopted Buddhism. Called To in Japan, these towers, symbolic of Buddhist cosmology, were built usually in three, five, or seven receding stages or stories, retaining the stepped stone base and nine-ringed top mast of the original *stupas*. Pagodas in Japan have withstood centuries of earth tremor, their stability belied by their architectural form, yet assured by an unusual structural device. This is the large central post, sometimes resting on a stone base in the interior but frequently hanging from the upper beams, which acts during earthquakes as a sort of stabilizing pendulum for the entire structure, which rocks back and forth on its base.

7. Entasis, the convex curve in the outline of a column, typical of Greek columns of the Doric order especially, may be due to the influence of architecture at Gandhara, the site of a Greek colony of Hellenic times on the northwest coast of what is now India. Decorative motifs on roof tiles at Horyuji also seem to show Greek influence.

8. The Daibutsuden still requires considerable effort. The last restoration in 1913 required a quarter of a million man-days. Previously the building was burned down twice, in 1180 and

1567, and then rebuilt. The great Buddha was cast seven times before it was successfully completed in 752; its head melted off in the first fire, was shaken off twice by earthquakes, and appears now as restored in 1692.

9. Nearby concrete buildings are the scene of restoration work on the more fragile treasures of the Shosoin which are kept there in consideration of the dust-producing effects of contemporary motor traffic.

10. Counted among the reasons for the move from Nara may be the Todaiji priesthood's extending its growing power into secular affairs, the desire by a new lineage of the Imperial family to mark their accession to the throne with a new capital, perhaps even the desire to move from the location where sickness in the Imperial family was attributed to the avenging spirit of a prince who died after being exiled. There were in fact two moves, one to a location near Kyoto where a new capital was begun and almost completed and then a sudden move to the nearby site of Heian-kyo (Kyoto) in 793.

11. The word *shoin* can refer to the desk alcove itself (the original meaning), to the room in which a desk alcove is located, or to the style of architecture which incorporated both desk and room.

12. Construction of the Japanese "House in the Garden" at New York's Museum of Modern Art in 1953 was based on two almost identical Shoin buildings of the early seventeenth century, both at the Onjoji Temple in Otsu. The one illustrated here is the Kyakuden (Guest House) of the Kojoin Temple, a subsidiary temple at Onjoji.

13. Among them were Fushimi Castle at Momoyama, now gone, and Osaka Castle, a huge construction enclosing 100 acres, the encircling moats about 120 feet wide, the escarpments a demonstration of expert civil engineering. Some of the stone blocks are equivalent to railroad cars in size and volume. Osaka Castle was burned during a siege in 1615 and again in 1868. The present structure is a reinforced-concrete reconstruction.

14. Valuable rocks were often wrapped during transport and any moss on them was carefully watered en route. Bridges were strengthened to bear their weight. The Japanese feeling for rocks is akin to the Western regard for sculpture. A rock dealer's establishment resembles an art gallery with stones

displayed for perusal, their aesthetic attributes and pedigree being a matter for serious critical discussion.

15. *Japan: The Official Guide* (1954 edition, p. 236) gives the all-too-perfect definition for the contemporary tea ceremony: "...an esthetic cult in vogue among polite circles in Japan, where it is regarded as an institution of disciplinary training for the promotion of enlightenment and mental composure."

# CHRONOLOGY

*Chronological Divisions of Japanese Architectural History
(according to Professor Jiro Murata, Kyoto University)*

| | |
|---|---|
| JOKO | —ca. 550 |
| ASUKA | ca.550– 644 |
| (EARLY NARA | 645– 707 |
| (NARA (TEMPYO) | 708– 793 |
| (EARLY HEIAN | 794– 897 |
| (HEIAN (FUJIWARA) | 898–1185 |
| KAMAKURA | 1186–1335 |
| MUROMACHI | 1336–1573 |
| MOMOYAMA | 1573–1614 |
| EDO | 1615–1867 |
| MEIJI | 1868–1912 |
| TAISHO | 1913–1926 |
| SHOWA | 1926– |

*chashitsu* a small garden pavilion or a room within a house specifically designed for the tea ceremony.

*chigi* the continuation of crossed gable-end boards forming V-shape projections above the ridge of a Shinto shrine building.

*chumon* the "middle" or intermediate gate located between the outer south gate and the actual shrine or temple buildings.

*fusuma* sliding interior partitions made of a latticework wood frame covered with heavy opaque paper.

*haniwa* small clay representations of houses and figures found in archaic tombs, also placed around ancient Imperial burial mounds, possibly to prevent erosion.

*hibachi* a portable charcoal brazier used for warming the hands.

*hisashi* roofed verandas or corridors attached to the main rooms of a dwelling (usually not covered with *tatami*).

*honden* the central sanctuary building of a Shinto shrine which houses the representation of the deity.

*jodan* a raised area or platform within a room, on which *tokonoma*, *tana*, and *shoin* are usually located, designating the most important interior space.

*katsuogi* tapered wood cylinders along the ridges of Shinto shrine buildings.

118

*kondo* the "Golden Hall," or central sanctuary building, which usually houses the most sacred images of a Buddhist temple.

*moya* the central interior space of a Shinden.

*nageshi* horizontal wood plank or wide molding, usually near the top of a room, resembling a beam between posts.

*ramma* decoratively carved or openwork panels above sliding *fusuma* doors.

*shinden*  the chief building of a Heian Period mansion-estate; also *Shinden style*, the site arrangement and architectural characteristics of a Shinden and its subsidiary buildings.

*shitomido*  hinged paper-covered wood lattice "doors," swung up horizontally and hooked open, forming the façades of Shinden buildings.

*shoin*  a desk alcove projecting onto the veranda, with a *shoji* window above it; for *Shoin style* see note 11.

*shoji*  sliding outer partition "doors" made of a latticework wood frame and covered with translucent white paper, also used in walls as sliding "windows."

*sudare*  horizontal roll-up bamboo blinds made of thin bamboo strips.

*sukiya*  an elaborate *chashitsu* (more like a pavilion) for the tea ceremony; also Sukiya *style* which refers to a refinement of the usual architectural elements in this type of building.

*tainoya*  pavilions containing subsidiary living quarters and located on either side of the central house, or Shinden, in Shinden style architecture.

*tatami*  rectangular rush-covered floor mats approximately six-by-three feet in size and about two inches thick; the edges on the long sides are bound by cloth strips.

*tateana*  prehistoric thatch roofed pit-dwellings.

*tokonoma*  the recessed alcove, in a room, used specifically for the display of paintings, ceramics, flower arrangements, and other forms of art.

*torii*  the entrance "gate" to a Shinto shrine (see note 5).

*tsuridono*  a small open pavilion set over the garden pond in a Shinden style estate and used as a place for aesthetic diversion.

*watadono*  the corridors connecting the Shinden and *tainoya* in Shinden style architecture.

# BIBLIOGRAPHY

Akiyama, Aisaburo, *Shinto and its Architecture*, Kinki Kanko Kyokai, Kyoto, 1936.

Blaser, Werner, *Japanese Temples and Tea Houses*, F. W. Dodge, New York, 1956.

Carver, Norman H., *Form and Space of Japanese Architecture*, Shokokusha, Tokyo, 1955.

Department of the Interior, Imperial Japanese Government, *Japanese Temples and their Treasures*, The Shimbi Shoin, Tokyo, 1910.

Drexler, Arthur, *The Architecture of Japan*, The Museum of Modern Art, New York, 1955.

Harada, Jiro, *The Lesson of Japanese Architecture*, rev. ed., Charles T. Branford, Boston, 1954.

Ishimoto, Yasuhiro; Tange, Kenzo; Gropius, Walter, *Katsura: Tradition and Creation in Japanese Architecture*, Yale University Press, New Haven, 1960.

*Japanese Scroll Paintings*, Kodokawa, Tokyo, 1958.

Kitao, Harumichi, *Famous Ancient Houses in Japan (Kokuho Shoin Zushu)*, 13 vols., Kyosha, Tokyo, 1938–40.

Koike, Shinji, *Contemporary Architecture of Japan*, Shokokusha, Tokyo, 1954.

Kokusai Bunka Shinkokai (The Society for International Cultural Relations), *Architectural Beauty in Japan*, The Studio Publications, New York, 1936.

Kultermann, Udo, *New Japanese Architecture*, F. A. Praeger, New York, 1960.

Morse, Edward S., *Japanese Homes and their Surroundings*, Ticknor and Company, Boston, 1886. (Reprinted by Dover Publications, New York, 1961.)

——, *Japan Day by Day*, Harper & Bros., New York, 1889.

Okakura, Kakuzo, *The Book of Tea*, Fox Duffield and Co., New York, 1912.

——, *The Ideals of the East*, E. P. Dutton & Co., New York, 1920.

Ota, Hakutaro, *Zuseki Nihon Jutaku Shi (History of Japanese Domestic Architecture)*, Shokokusha, Tokyo, 1952 (in Japanese).

Paine, Robert T.; Soper, Alexander C., *The Art and Architecture of Japan*, Penguin Books, Middlesex, 1955.

Sadler, A. L., *Chanoyu, the Japanese Tea Ceremony*, J. L. Thompson & Co., Ltd., Kobe (?), 1934.

——, *A Short History of Japanese Architecture*, Angus and Robertson, Sydney, 1941.

Sansom, George B., *Japan: a Short Cultural History*, rev. ed., The Cresset Press, London, 1952.

Sen, Soshitsu; Murata, Jiro; Kitamura, Denbe, *Chashitsu: Original Drawings and Photographic Illustrations of Typical Japanese Tea Architecture and Gardens*, Tanka-Shinsha Co., Kyoto, 1959.

Soper, Alexander C., *The Evolution of Buddhist Architecture in Japan*, Princeton University Press, Princeton, 1942.

Staff of Tokyo National Museum, *Pageant of Japanese Art*, Toto Bunka Co., Tokyo, 1952 (Vol. 6, *Architecture and Gardens*).

Taut, Bruno, *Houses and People of Japan*, 2nd ed., Sanseido, Tokyo, 1958.

——, *Fundamentals of Japanese Architecture*, Kokusai Bunka Shinkokai, Tokyo, 1936.

Tamura, Tsuyoshi, *Art of the Landscape Garden in Japan*, Kokusai Bunka Shinkokai, Tokyo, 1935.

Terry, T. Philip, *Terry's Japanese Empire* ("A Guidebook for Travelers"), Houghton Mifflin Company, Boston and New York, 1914.

Yoshida, Tetsuro, *Das Japanisches Wohnhaus*, Wasmuth, Berlin, 1935.

——, *The Japanese House and Garden*, F. A. Praeger, New York, 1955.

*(In addition to sources included above, the author has drawn heavily on the text for the exhibition entitled* The Architecture of Japan *which he prepared and organized in 1953 for circulation by the International Program of the New York Museum of Modern Art.)*

# INDEX

Numbers in **regular roman** type refer to text pages; *italic* figures refer to the plates.

123

# SOURCES OF ILLUSTRATIONS

Alex, William, New York City: 8, 12, 105, 110, 112, 114, 116

Aoi, T, Asahi Shimbun, Tokyo: 128, 129

Department of the Interior, Imperial Japanese Government, in *Japanese Temples and their Treasures* (Tokyo, 1910): 15a, 15b, 17, 18, 19a, 19b, 25, 33, 35, 36, 46, 54, 58, 59

Ishimoto, Yasuhiro, Kanagawa-ken, Japan: 115, 118, 142; in Ishimoto, Tange and Gropius, *Katsura: Tradition and Creation in Japanese Architecture*, Yale University Press (New Haven, 1960): 131, 132, 133, 134, 135, 138, 139, 140, 145

Japanese Tourist Association, Tokyo: 22, 104, 141

Courtesy of Kadokawa Publishing Company, Tokyo in *Japanese Scroll Paintings* (1958), Vol. II: 39, 68; Vol. X: 78

*Koku Kuwa Yobu* (Tokyo, 1883): 9, 10

Kokusai Bunka Shinkokai (The Society for International Cultural Relations), Tokyo: Photogrammetric Company: 6; Mainichi Newspaper Company: 7; Y. Watanabe: 11, 13, 14, 43, 106, 113, 151; T. Sato: 53, 65, 66, 67, 69, 70, 72, 83, 85, 94, 130, 144; in Tamura Tsuyoshi, *Art of the Landscape Garden in Japan* (1935): 117; T, Kato: 123; F. Muraswa: 152, 153

Courtesy of Kyosha Publishing Company, Tokyo, in Kitao, Harumichi, *Kokuho Shoin Zushu* (Famous Ancient Houses in Japan) (1938–40), Vol. X: 80, 82, 84; Vol. XI: 125, 126

Courtesy of National Treasures Buildings Publishing Committee, Tokyo in *Kokuho Kenzo Butsu* (National Treasures Buildings) (1933–36): 28, 29, 30, 37, 38, 40, 41, 44, 45, 47, 55, 56, 87, 88, 89, 90, 91, 92, 93

F. A. Praeger, New York, in Yoshida, Tetsuro, *The Japanese House and Garden* (1955): 74, 75

Shokokusha Publishing Company, Tokyo, in Ota, Hakutaro, *Nihon Jutaku Shi* (History of Japanese Domestic Architecture) (1952): 1, 2, 3, 4, 60, 61, 64, 71, 73, 81, 101; in *Nihon Kenchiku* (Japanese Architecture) (1941–43): 16, 48, 49, 50, 51, 52, 96, 97, 98, 120, 122, 148, 149, 150; S. F. Murasawa: 31, 32, 34, 95

Tange, Kenzo, *A Plan for Tokyo*, 1960 (Tokyo, 1961): 154

Tokyo National Museum, Tokyo: 5b; courtesy of Benrido Company, Kyoto: 5a

Courtesy of Tokyo News Service, Ltd., Tokyo, in Akiyama, Aisaburo, *Shinto and its Architecture* (Kyoto, 1936): 20a, 20b, 21a, 21b

Courtesy of Toto Bunka Publishing Company, Tokyo, in Tokyo National Museum (ed.), *Pageant of Japanese Art* (1952) Vol. VI: 15c, 19c, 20c, 21c, 57

Courtesy of Zauho Press, Tokyo, in *Juraku* (1930): 79, 99, 100, 102, 103, 107, 108, 109, 111, 119, 121, 124, 127, 136, 137, 143, 146, 147

Courtesy of Zokeisha Publications, Ltd., Tokyo: 42